Ecofundamentalism

Ecofundamentalism

A Critique of
Extreme Environmentalism

Rögnvaldur Hannesson

LEXINGTON BOOKS
Lanham • Boulder • New York • Toronto • Plymouth, UK

Published by Lexington Books
A wholly owned subsidiary of Rowman & Littlefield
4501 Forbes Boulevard, Suite 200, Lanham, Maryland 20706
www.rowman.com

10 Thornbury Road, Plymouth PL6 7PP, United Kingdom

British Library Cataloguing in Publication Information Available

Library of Congress Cataloging-in-Publication Data

Library of Congress Cataloging-in-Publication Data Available
ISBN: 978-0-7391-8963-4 (cloth : alk. paper)
ISBN: 978-0-7391-8964-1 (electronic)

♾™ The paper used in this publication meets the minimum requirements of American
National Standard for Information Sciences—Permanence of Paper for Printed Library
Materials, ANSI/NISO Z39.48-1992.

Printed in the United States of America

Contents

Acknowledgment

This book was finalized while I was Julian Simon fellow at the Property and Environment Research Center (PERC) in Bozeman, Montana, August to October 2013. I am grateful to the researchers I met at PERC for constructive and stimulating discussions on some topics raised in the book. The book is meant to be in Julian Simon's spirit; something he would agree with if he were still around. The ultimate responsibility for what the book has to say rests, needless to say, only with myself.

Rögnvaldur Hannesson

Chapter One

Introduction

After thirty years in the environmental movement, I am worried that as it gains power it cares less and less about reason and science. Its influence on movies, academia, and literature has already turned history into fiction and propaganda. . . . In short I believe the environmental movement has almost lost touch with reality.

—Former environmental activist Wallace Kaufman (1994), p. 7

One caveman says to another: "Something's just not right—our air is clean, our water is pure, we all get plenty of exercise, everything we eat is organic and free-range, and yet nobody lives past thirty."

—Alex Gregory, cartoon in the *New Yorker*, May 22, 2006

"A specter is haunting Europe," wrote Karl Marx and Friedrich Engels in their *Communist Manifesto* in 1848, "the specter of communism." The specter was a force to be reckoned with for a long time. Then, at the end of the twentieth century, it was laid to rest, as the Soviet Union collapsed and communism proved to be an utterly unsuitable blueprint for social and economic organization.

In modern times, another specter is haunting not just Europe but the world at large, the specter of environmentalism. It has certain similarities to, but is also different from, the specter of communism. Socialism or communism—the distinction is not always clear—arose from large differences in material well-being. The industrial revolution brought legions of poor people from the land to the cities to work in factories. For many, and probably most, the factories were an improvement over whatever living they could eke out on the land. That did not necessarily sooth their frustration because, compared

1

with their masters, factory workers' living standard was low indeed. The willingness to change things, by violent means if necessary, does not arise from misery as such; it arises from the perception that things can be improved. The changes brought about by the industrial revolution certainly brought home the point that change was possible, and the wealth created by the new factories was a manifestation that living conditions for the proletariat could be improved if only it were distributed more evenly.

The specter of environmentalism has a different origin. It did not arise from the frustrations of the downtrodden. Instead, it arose from a bad conscience of the pampered. Environmentalism is not an ideology justifying the struggle of the poor for a better lot, it is a malaise among those who have enough or more than enough.

There is another way in which socialism and environmentalism differ from one another. Socialism is a child of the Enlightenment. It sprang from a belief in science as a vehicle for human progress, from an understanding that science and technology would provide the material abundance needed to lift humanity from misery. That notwithstanding, it turned out to be gravely mistaken. Nevertheless, it is to the scientists and philosophers of the Enlightenment that we owe the replacement of superstition with scientific inquiry and the use of science for human progress; indeed we are still drawing on that inheritance. Environmentalism is of a different kind. Even if it is often dressed up in scientific garb, its most extreme variety incorporates deep skepticism toward science, taking its cue from nature mysticism. This skepticism manifests itself in skepticism about any interference with nature; it is as if nature knows best. Reduced to its absurd consequences, this type of environmentalism tells us that humanity should never have entered the stone age and made tools; we should still be gathering fruit and killing animals we could handle with our bare hands. Presumably no one in his right mind would want to go that far, but it is entirely unclear where to draw the line. Should we still be hunters and gatherers, but using stone tools? Should we just have avoided artificial fertilizer? Or pesticides? Or coal and oil?

This book is a critique of environmentalism of this kind. Environmentalism is a very broad concept. Some people talk about "the environmental movement" as if it were a unified force striving toward a common goal. This is far from being true. People who call themselves environmentalists hold very different views on what it means and strive toward different and often competing goals. Many, perhaps most, are against nuclear energy, others see it as the only credible way of reducing carbon dioxide emissions without depriving us of the energy use essential for our way of life. Many, perhaps most, see global warming as a threat, but some think it is an overblown issue and still care for wildlife and other issues of environmental concern. Criticizing environmentalism is not a fight against a many-headed hydra, it is more like fighting against some ideas that are ill taken while supporting others that are constructive and strive for a better world.

So what is good and what is bad about environmentalism? We all depend ultimately on nature. Environmentalism in the sense of taking care of nature so that we can live better is, needless to say, a good thing. But there is another type of environmentalism, one that puts nature above man, one that would sacrifice our way of life if it in any sense conflicts with nature as its proponents see it. This book seeks to debunk this kind of environmentalism, expose its inner contradictions and the threat it ultimately poses against our way of life and civilization. This kind of environmentalism may well be a minority or even marginal opinion, but there are signs that this mind-set has more influence and penetrates people's way of thinking to a greater extent than it deserves. This mind-set makes otherwise reasonable people receptive to exaggerated or plainly wrong arguments against nuclear energy, use of fossil fuels, genetically modified foods, opening up of new mines, and much else. It makes people predisposed to support, by donating money and otherwise, organizations that claim they are trying to save the world when in reality they would be better described as trying to destroy it. One may wonder at which point in our history we would be stuck if this mind-set had guided the decisions of our forefathers. It is this kind of environmentalism I am criticizing and for which I often shall, for brevity, use the terms environmentalism and environmentalists without further qualification. There is an additional reason for that. Sadly to say, more often than not it is this type of environmentalism that the media refer to when they write or talk about "the environmental movement."

I begin by discussing what environmentalism is (chapter 2). Is it ideology or religion or a bit of both? It has no pope and no churches. Like socialism it is a political program, but much more diffuse. As already indicated there are two strands of environmentalism, "wise use" environmentalism that strives to take care of nature in our own interest, and ecofundamentalism, or "deep ecology," that puts nature above man. Not only does ecofundamentalism run counter to human history, in its logical extreme it could well be the end of history. Those who call themselves environmentalists are not necessarily either one or the other of these two extremes but somewhere in between. This book is about which of the two extremes they would do well to avoid.

Ideology or religion, whatever it is, environmentalist writings typically have a strong element of faith. The world is set on a disastrous course if their warnings are not heeded. Not only are there unconditional predictions about future developments that are difficult to predict, but even about things we have no way of knowing with any degree of certainty. According to *The*

Limits to Growth we should now have run out of oil or drowned in our own pollution, and probably both, or at the very least be close to it. But we have never had much idea about how much oil there is in the ground, or mineral resources. Not only would it be prohibitively expensive to find out quickly, but it is essentially unknowable, because it depends on unknowable technological progress, as the recent shale oil and gas revolution has demonstrated; this revolution is due to technological progress and took even well-informed commentators by surprise. Overpopulation has been touted as a major threat ever since Malthus. Later prophets of overpopulation do not have the excuse of Malthus, whose analysis was basically correct for the world as it was up to his time; his life coincided with the rise of the industrial revolution in England, and he did not have the benefit of looking back on decades of technological progress making a mockery of the notion of a stagnant society. Yet modern day Malthusians like Paul Ehrlich show no sign of revising their conclusions after decades of development counter to their predictions have turned them to ridicule. The jury is still out on the global warming scaremongers, but there is more than a fair chance that they will turn out to be victims of disaster results that are pre-programmed into their computers without much basis in reality. All these issues are prominent among the delusions of environmentalism and discussed in later chapters.

Boiled down to its essentials, environmentalism is about our relationship with nature. One of the tenets of environmentalism is that we have outgrown the bounds nature sets to our existence, that our civilization and way of life are not sustainable. This is the subject of chapter 3. The concept of sustainability can be traced to *The Limits to Growth* and on to *Our Common Future*. This cherished concept does not get us very far, however. Our use of nonrenewable resources is by definition not sustainable. Even for renewable resources the concept of sustainability gives very limited guidance. Nice as it may sound, it is perhaps best forgotten. The chapter ends with a discussion of the precautionary principle, more adequately named the paralyzing principle. As Cass Sunstein has put it, "it bans every imaginable step, including inaction itself."[1]

Biodiversity is a notion that, together with sustainability and the precautionary principle, has become one of those code words of environmentalism that are supposed to suffice to close any argument. Anything that is not sustainable, precautionary, or that harms biodiversity is supposed to be bad and not needing further discussion. But code words cannot replace analysis. What does biodiversity mean? Is less biodiversity always and everywhere a bad thing? Should biodiversity be maintained at any price? This is the subject of chapter 4.

Prolific use of energy is perhaps what more than anything characterizes modern civilization. But the fact that most of our energy use is patently unsustainable and has been so for a long time underlines how little by way of useful advice the concept of sustainability has to offer. It asks the wrong question. The relevant questions are how much do we have of unsustainable sources of energy, how long will they last, and could they be replaced? Unfortunately, no one knows the answers to these questions, nor is it likely that anyone can come up with reliable answers to them that are valid for the long term. Technological progress, as already argued, is unknowable, and the abundance of nonrenewable resources depends on technological progress. Iron ore or oil in the ground are both useless in and of themselves; it is our technology and how it enables us to use them that make them valuable. And it is also technology that determines where and whether we can access them and how much we can get out of the ground. Chapter 5 discusses energy issues and argues that the much touted renewable energy is highly unlikely to satisfy modern civilization's need for energy, let alone the development needs of the poor countries of the world.

The energy issues are pertinent partly because of the alleged risk of global warming. Is it happening, is it man-made, what are the consequences, and what can we do about them? The uncertainty increases with every question. Global warming has been going on since the end of the Little Ice Age, but to what extent is it man-made? Is it just one of those natural climate fluctuations that have always occurred? The Little Ice Age was not a happy time, and global warming has already brought benefits, but what if the warming continues? Humans have spread themselves into almost every nook and cranny of the globe and so seem fairly independent of climate except for growing their food. That is, needless to say, critical, but moderate warming would probably make that easier, if anything. The issue of global warming is one of heated debates and much controversy. It has certain parallels with the issue of forest death, much hyped in the 1980s, and the ozone hole. All of these are discussed in chapter 6.

The notion that humanity has outgrown the bounds set by the planet can be seen as a question of whether there are too many of us. Many environmentalists maintain with gusto that we are far too many. Chapter 7 deals with population growth and whether or not it might be self-correcting, and whether or not we will be able to continue to feed ourselves. Despite strong statements by environmentalists and others, no one knows the answers to these questions, but there are some encouraging clues.

World fisheries are one source of our food. They are not the most important one; between 6 and 7 percent of the world's protein comes from fish,[2] but in some areas fish is the most important source of food. Nevertheless they deserve a chapter of their own, as they have received much attention by environmentalists. The prevailing idea seems to be that things are going from bad to worse and have been doing so for a long time. But in what sense? Many environmentalists seem more preoccupied with the world's oceans as a gigantic theme park than as a source of food. Aquaculture often meets with skepticism or outright opposition from environmentalists. Chapter 8 discusses the status of world fisheries and the place of aquaculture in feeding the world population, which as we all know is still rising.

Finally there is a concluding chapter. It pulls together the threads from previous chapters and pays homage to Bjørn Lomborg's book *The Skeptical Environmentalist*. This book does not try to replicate his painstaking investigation, but seeks to debunk environmentalism of the ecofundamentalist variety as ahistorical, unscientific, and an outright threat to our further progress.

NOTES

1. Sunstein (2002), p. 104.
2. According to FAO (2012), p. 5.

Chapter Two

Environmentalism: What Is It?

The Greater Yellowstone is the nation's medicine bundle. It must remain whole and intact. Let us send up our prayers, remembering the grizzly, remembering the wolf, remembering the white wings of the trumpeter swans. May we never forget each pilgrimage is holy.

—Environmentalist Rick Reese, quoted in Fitzsimmons (1999), p. 72

By exploitation of the world's resources on a purely extractive basis [humans have] postponed the meeting at the ecological judgment seat . . .. The Day of Judgment is at hand.

—William Vogt (1948), *Road to Survival*, p. 78

Like socialism, environmentalism is a very wide concept. The most extreme varieties of socialism turned out to be literally lethal, while the milder ones have their positive attributes. The modern welfare state can be traced to socialist ideas, even if its very beginnings were in imperial Germany under Bismarck, who was anything but a socialist. Likewise there are different kinds of environmentalism. "Wise use" environmentalism acknowledges the fact that we are where we are because we have conquered nature, to the extent it can be conquered, learnt her laws and turned them to our own advantage. But we need to do this wisely so that we do not destroy the very basis of our existence. We need to clean up the mess we leave behind. This kind of environmentalism takes care of nature in our own interest. Who could be against that?

By contrast, ecofundamentalism, or "deep ecology," sees nature as paramount. Humanity is a part of nature, and we have to follow her laws, not tinker with them and turn them to our own advantage. The problem with this

7

is that it threatens modern civilization and its way of life. Humanity has long since outgrown its place in the pristine ecology of the planet. We have been able to do this because we have changed our surroundings beyond recognition to grow our food. We have uprooted the plants that used to grow on the land and replaced them with vast monocultures, aided by fertilizers and pest control. We have selectively bred our domesticated animals to suit our needs, and few if any of them would survive in nature on their own. Living in harmony with nature, as the deep ecologists suggest, is utterly incompatible with this. Nevertheless, many if not most of the high priests of deep ecology seem quite happy to avail themselves of the fruits of modern civilization; they fly around the world to confer with the like-minded, they eat what they can buy in the supermarket, and live in comfortable dwellings with heating or cooling, or both, depending on where they are.

Given that so many ardent environmentalists are unwilling to practice what they preach, it is tempting to dismiss their preachings as just so much hot air. Their inconsistencies do not promote confidence in the message, and then there is the silliness of the message itself. But that view is too optimistic. Eco-fundamentalism seems to influence the mind-set of many people, even if its most extreme varieties have a negligible following. That mind-set often gets in the way of policies that support or enhance our standard of living; it gets in the way of drilling for oil in areas perceived as important for wild animals, and it has been an obstacle for modern biotechnology. It prevents building of dams for hydroelectric power or even encourages their dismantling for the sake of a few fish; over the period 1980–2006 the hydropower capacity in the United States declined by five percent.[1] For those who see modern civilization as an achievement and worth promoting, fighting the extremes of environmentalism and exposing its fallacies certainly is not only worthwhile, it may be an act of self-preservation.

The rhetoric of extreme environmentalism postulates that humans are just a part of the ecology and that the "problem" is that we have far outgrown the place the ecological balance would put us in. It is difficult to find a position that would be more at odds with human history and achievements, not just since the industrial revolution but indeed since our ancestors began to experiment with agriculture. This is not a rhetorical exaggeration; Dave Foreman, a deep ecologist and one-time board member of the Sierra Club, has said that the "nascency of agriculture" about 10,000 years ago set us "apart from the natural world" and resulted in the evils of "city, bureaucracy, patriarchy, war and empire."[2] Even back in the stone age humanity was somewhat out of kilt with the ecological balance; our ancestors made tools to enhance their chances of survival. Then came selective breeding of plants and domestication of animals, all interfering with the pristine ecological balance. But the industrial revolution topped it all by far. In fact, "industrial" revolution is a bit of a misnomer; what happened was that muscle power, both from humans and animals, was replaced by power from fossil fuels, via the steam engine. Even if the steam engine has run its course, literally and metaphorically, we still are critically dependent on fossil fuels for our way of life and likely to remain so for the foreseeable future, as will be discussed in a later chapter.

How the exploitative and investigative attitude toward nature is the key to our well-being was well put by a perceptive Chinese observer in the aftermath of the industrial revolution. China was, arguably, the richest and most advanced country in the world up to the industrial revolution. Then, to their great surprise and chagrin, the Chinese were superseded by and dictated to by the British and other powerful western nations. Liu Xihong, visiting England in 1876, put it this way: "It is not that our emperors or prime ministers of each dynasty were less intelligent than the Westerners, but none among them strove to open up the skies or dig up the earth to compete with nature for enriching themselves."[3] More than a hundred years later the Chinese have evidently learned the lesson while much of the western world seems to have forgotten it.

IDEOLOGY OR RELIGION?

How could environmentalism arise? And what is it? Is it ideology or religion, or a mixture of both? How dangerous is it? The origin and ascendancy of ideas and ideologies is a complex phenomenon for which no one has a good explanation. How could Christianity take over the Roman Empire? Christians at the time were a highly idiosyncratic sect, or multiple sects rather. Their superstitions were not an obvious improvement on the superstitions of the Roman religion. Perhaps the decisive things Christianity had to offer were exclusive zeal, an impending Day of Judgment, and salvation of the true believers.[4] As it superseded the pagan religion, Christianity adopted many of the pagan customs, such as cultivation of saints and their relics; in Gibbon's words, "the victors themselves [the Christians] were insensibly subdued by the arts of their vanquished rivals."[5] There often is a greater continuity across revolutions than we are inclined to believe.

Constantine, the first Christian emperor, found Christianity useful is his fight against his challengers and may have believed its tenets, but was prudent enough not to be baptized until so late in his life that he had few or no more opportunities to sin.[6] Both he and later emperors are likely to have found a religion with a single god demanding unstinting obedience congenial for an empire ruled by a despot; later the kings of Europe referred to themselves as regents by the grace of god. Christianity did not strengthen the Roman Empire; ever since Gibbon put forward the thesis in *The Decline and Fall of the Roman Empire*, many have believed that it helped bring the empire down. How so? Hugh Trevor-Roper's summary of Gibbon is not without relevance in the present context:

> In particular, as a cause and symptom of corruption, Gibbon singled out monasticism. . . . It withdrew the resources of society, both human and economic, from that free and useful circulation on which progress depended. It condemned men to idleness, immobilized wealth, kept land in mortmain. And it positively undermined the very idea of civic virtue.[7]

By contrast, the adoption of Islam by the tribes of Arabia ushered in a wave of Arab conquests over vast territories in Africa and Asia, even if it is difficult to see in what way Islam is any better than its close cousin Christianity. Islam may at that time have been superior as a warrior religion, but surely Christianity made its strides as such later on, and seems in fact already to have done so when it was adopted by Emperor Constantine.

The ascendancy of Christianity and Islam lies in the distant past and we have only limited documentation about how the two came to their conquests. This is not the case with environmentalism; even if its roots can be traced back for a hundred years or more, it has mainly risen to prominence in the last four decades or so. What sets the last four decades or so apart from previous periods in human history is the level of affluence in the rich countries of the world. Environmentalism was begotten of affluence. Environmentalism really took hold in the late 1960s and early 1970s as a reaction to the golden age of economic growth in the western world after the Second World War. As the one time British Prime Minister Harold Macmillan famously put it, "you have never had it so good." In Western Europe and North America, material well-being had reached unparalleled heights by the late 1960s and reached even the common man and woman. More and more people began thinking about other things in life. And there were downsides to high material standards that were less obvious earlier; pollution of the atmosphere, lakes and rivers, and less and less pristine areas left. Out of this, and a hodgepodge of ideas about man's relations with nature, untrustworthiness of politicians, and much else, environmentalist ideas came to the fore and came to be promoted by organizations of various kinds (Greenpeace, Friends of the Earth, the World Wildlife Fund, the Sierra Club, to name a few). This setting provided opportunities for charismatic and enterprising individuals to make a living from catering to the superstitions of a gullible public, much as other preachers, prophets, and evangelists of various kinds, often famous for other things than practicing what they preach.

Defining environmentalism is elusive, however. The concept is extremely broad and in fact encompasses views that often are hard to reconcile. Many authors and commentators talk and write about the Environmental Movement in the determinate singular, as if it were a monolithic movement striving toward a common goal. This is misleading, if not plain wrong. Environmentalists often are at each other's throats. It is true that violent disagreements in exclusive sects often arise over minor differences; sometimes the greater the vehemence the harder it is, for an outsider anyway, to perceive what the disagreement is all about. Ideological fights among leftist sects provide many amusing examples. But among people who would identify themselves as environmentalists the disagreements are often real and founded in substantial differences in outlook. Most environmentalists probably agree on the perils of greenhouse gas emissions from fossil fuels, but while some regard nuclear power as the only credible solution, others oppose it vehemently and believe solar and wind power will suffice. And it is unclear how far one should go in living in harmony with nature. Does an environmentalist have to be vegetarian? Can he or she eat fruit and vegetables transported over long distances? And then there are the wise use types who want to take care of nature in our own interest and would loath to be bundled together with the ecofundamentalists.

But what distinguishes ideology from religion? Both incorporate a set of beliefs and maxims of behavior. An ideology such as socialism postulates that humanity should direct its efforts at satisfying human needs and distribute the fruits of this endeavor fairly amongst all of us. "From each according to ability and to each according to need" is a way it has been put. A nice idea, but problems arise as soon as we try to put it into practice. There are innumerable ways of doing so and still stay within the ideological confines of socialism, as witnessed by the plethora of political parties and sects that have characterized themselves as socialist. And what distinguishes Christianity, or Islam, or any other of the world's religions? All incorporate rules of human behavior and beliefs about how the world came about and what is the ultimate arbiter of right and wrong. All religions are sufficiently obscure to encompass a multitude of sub-classes and sects, all equally sure that they have the correct interpretation of the message. Christians are divided into Roman Catholics, Orthodox, innumerable Protestant sects, and more. Muslims are divided into Sunnis and Shias and more, and so on. And not to forget, Christians have fought other Christians and Muslims other Muslims with vehemence and violence, ostensibly over minor doctrinaire differences, but probably more often over differences in material interests so disguised.

If there is anything that distinguishes ideologies from religions it is that a religion has at its core a belief in something supernatural. Christians, Muslims, and Jews all share a common god, but seldom happily, whose existence can neither be proven nor refuted. The Hindus have several hundreds of them, which would seem to go well with modern ideas of consumer choice. Many socialists have regarded their ideology as atheist. It is certainly true that socialism does not seek its legitimacy in supernatural beliefs, but it is nevertheless a set of beliefs about how societies should be governed, and even though some socialists have regarded their creed as "scientific" there is nothing scientific about it. Egalitarianism is a nice idea, but cannot be proven right or wrong. It may be argued that socialism is patently unscientific to the extent it believes that humans are motivated by compassion for their fellow beings and not by pursuing one's self-interest; the attempts that have been made at putting socialism into practice have generated cliques of self-serving usurpers who evidently had other things than the well-being of "the masses" on their minds. Like religion, ideologies such as socialism are based on beliefs about human nature and how we should organize our societies, the difference being that the basis for these beliefs is not sought in something supernatural. There have indeed been many individuals who have characterized themselves as "Christian" socialists and pointed out that the maxims of socialism, which pertain to social organization, are not at odds with a belief in God or any other supernatural things.

Environmentalism is a curious mixture of ideology and religion. It is also a curious mixture of nature mystique, science, and anti-science. Many scientists do, and with reason, call themselves environmentalists. There is in fact something called environmental science, dealing with how our activities affect our environment and the limits that nature sets to what we can do. Releasing fumes and gases into the atmosphere may affect the climate, and acid rain, caused by emissions of sulfur dioxide, affects the growth of plants and even fish in freshwater lakes. Release of sewage into streams and lakes causes excessive growth of algae, which ultimately may deplete fish populations. Growing our food ultimately relies on the fertility of the soil, which could be harmed by excessive fertilization, use of pesticides, and irrigation. True, our civilization could not exist without massive interfering with natural processes, but just as clearly could we harm ourselves if we did not do so with care and thorough knowledge of the natural processes on which we rely. Knowledge of such processes and intelligent interference with them is wise use environmentalism.

But there is more to it than that. Many environmentalists, and certainly the most outspoken ones, would be outraged by having themselves described as advocates for wise use of nature. For them, nature is above human civilization; man has to find his place in nature (the most politically correct among them would probably say woman has to find her place in nature), and nothing would be worse than trying to tinker with the processes of nature in order to carve out a greater living space. This is the worldview of the ecofundamentalists. In this worldview, curiously, science has taken the place of the unscientific and supernatural. Rather than using our scientific knowledge to improve our living conditions, as humanity has traditionally done, we are supposed to use it as a tool for the opposite, for letting the processes of nature run their course, for not cutting down trees to build our homes and make our furniture, for leaving plants and animals alone rather than cultivate those that best suit our needs, to say nothing of extracting oil and minerals. This is not a caricature; these are indeed the tenets of the most extreme form of environmentalism, what has become known as "deep ecology." Anyone will be hard put to find anything more antihuman than this set of ideas. These conceptions are sufficiently widespread to have generated a market for publications such as Alan Weisman's book *The World without Us*, which deals with how the world would return to its pristine state once humanity had been taken out.

Needless to say, the deep ecologists have not found it easy to live in harmony with their preachings. Some of them go to quite some length to do so, but it is safe to say that their rituals rest on the ultimate support of modern civilization which they pretend to so much dislike. Some time ago the *New York Times* reported on a young artist couple trying to live an ecologically correct life. They were concerned with saving the forests and refused to use paper for their personal hygiene—the report hinted at the gory details. Maybe they bought ecological food, but they lived in an apartment in New York City.

In the English-speaking world, and the United States in particular, the roots of environmentalism can be traced to nature mystics such as Henry Thoreau, John Muir, and Aldo Leopold. They, and many others before and after, found beauty in nature, not least in its intricate complexities. But beauty is in the eye of the beholder. We do not know what goes on in the mind of a wolf, a dog, or a fly, but it is highly likely that this ability to perceive the beauty and complexity of nature is something only humans are capable of, and perhaps a luxury that we can indulge in once we have conquered nature to such an extent that our basic needs are satisfied. Rural landscapes are most beautiful in the eyes of those who do not have to make a living out of their often poor soil. Seen in that light, environmentalism, even in its weirdest manifestations, is a testimony to human achievement and man's special status in nature itself. Some environmentalists are prone to saying that the concept of humans as masters of the globe is a Judeo-Christian concept, on the authority of the Book of Genesis. It need not be; it is quite simply a result of human achievement and a testimony to human progress.

Some environmentalists have in fact characterized environmentalism as a new religion. In his book on Greenpeace, the former Greenpeace activist Rex

Weyler mentions pseudo-religious rituals administered by Bob Hunter, one of the founders of Greenpeace, who declared "ecology, it's our new religion." Greenpeace originated in Vancouver, Canada, among people who had made protests for various worthy causes a part of their lifestyle. In the beginning their primary concern was the nuclear bomb tests of the United States, which caused radioactive contamination of the atmosphere. Over time this metamorphosed into protests against various alleged abuses of nature. They found a highly lucrative arena in protests against seal and whale hunting. These activities were abhorrent to many well fed people in affluent societies, apparently untroubled by the fact that for their meals of beef and chicken they are indebted to the butcher's knife. Greenpeace and other activists apparently never found their way into a slaughterhouse to film what takes place there, but red seal blood on white snow made good pictures, and so did whale hunting, which Greenpeace activists also managed to film. Making seals and whales icons of undisturbed nature tapped well into the sentiments of the well fed and well off, who in no way depended on seal or whale hunting for their living. It also did wonders for the financing of Greenpeace. For the less well off seal hunters of Canada and Greenland it was a disaster, as it destroyed the market for their products.

Clearly there is a vast difference between the extremes of people who would call themselves environmentalists. At one extreme there are those who would go no further than saying that we have to utilize nature with intelligence and care and avoid irreversible damage when it is in our interest to do so. It would presumably be difficult to find anyone who would disagree with that. One might go as far as saying that this hardly merits being labeled as an ideology apart from ordinary common sense. At the other extreme there are those who would assign priority to unspoiled nature in every sense of the word. This is where we find the deep ecologists. Even they have made some compromises with the modern way of living, however unwillingly. But they would typically go very far in "minimizing the human footprint on nature," or "making nature a priority," as some of them would put it. They would assign value to nature for its own sake and not for the enjoyment or utility that humans would draw from nature. They see merit in predatory animals eating their prey rather than having the latter fall for the shot of a good marksman, or having the animal habitat being replaced by a cornfield or a dairy farm. But how far are they prepared to go? Does nature have any value beyond what humans assign to it, be it for their enjoyment or material benefit? The deep ecologists and especially people assigning "rights" akin to human rights to animals would say yes. Some of them would even do so for trees, living things but apparently unconscious, and for stones, mountains and rivers, inanimate things, irrespective of what we might think of them. This is ideology with more than a tinge of religion.

There is yet another way in which environmentalism resembles religion. All the world's great religions, Christianity in particular, have given rise to self-serving elites who make a living from what in the modern business lingo would be called "religious services." Hindu, Jain, and Buddhist temples have amassed enormous wealth and support armies of monks and prelates interpreting the sacred message. The Roman Catholic Church was and still is a formidable institution, supporting a mini-state with a large bureaucracy. The need to believe in supernatural and irrational forces is deep and widespread and a secure source of income for those who are willing and able to tap into it.

The irrationality environmentalists tap into, while often dressed in scientific language and half-truths, is not all that different. Many people can apparently be persuaded that modern civilization is not sustainable; that it is critically dependent on fossil energy resources which we are rapidly running out of and which use is changing the climate in ways that will bring disaster; that genetically engineered plants and animals are harmful "Frankenstein foods;" that the fish stocks of the oceans are being depleted rapidly; that we must preserve wild animals despite being a threat to humans where they occur. Tapping into these sentiments for donations has long since become big business and given rise to a profession sometimes called white-collar beggars. To further enhance those business opportunities these sentiments must be encouraged and supported by a suitable propaganda so that it becomes self-perpetuating. Fairly regularly many of us get unsolicited e-mails from organizations purporting to work for saving some animal species from extinction; some have been about sharks. "Sharks" is indeed an appropriate term to use for those most likely to benefit from the solicited donations; the shoals of environmental lawyers and lobbyists foraging in the "ecosystem" of environmental law and regulations.

The salvation offered by the fund-raisers of modern environmental organizations to a credulous public is not entirely different from what the ancient church offered the wealthy widows and spinsters of Rome as the West-Roman Empire approached its ignominious fall. In Gibbon's words:

> the females of noble and opulent houses possessed a very ample share of independent property, and many of those devout females had embraced the doctrines of Christianity, not only with the cold assent of understanding, but with the warmth of affection, and perhaps with the eagerness of fashion. . . . Some ecclesiastic, of real or apparent sanctity, was chosen to direct their timorous conscience, and to amuse the vacant tenderness of their heart . . .[8]

And then there are the modern indulgencies of carbon offsets sold to those who want to fly to their vacation destinations with a good conscience.

Many others have found parallels between environmentalism and religion, and between the biblical prophets and the modern environmental prophets.[9]

In 2003 Michael Crichton gave a lecture he entitled "Environmentalism as Religion."[10] He distinguished between science-based environmentalism and faith-based environmentalism. We need the former, but not the latter, and it is the latter that takes on the attributes of religion. Crichton's main concern was that environmentalists were perverting science to support positions based on faith. It is worse than that; some scientists actually morph into priests and present their faith as if it were science.

Wallace Kaufman, a former environmental activist who later began to be worried about the nature and influence of what he calls the environmental movement, puts it this way:

> Over the past twenty years the environmental meetings I attend as a journalist have seemed more and more like church meetings. Every year for five years I have sat with a group of widely published nature writers, most of them also respected lecturers and professors. These writers compile the anthologies that schools and universities use in courses on literature and the environment. This is a little like having a single religious sect write student textbooks. In our meetings, they talk about "converting" America and not letting science interfere with a "spiritual" understanding of nature. They talk about all creatures being "sacred." Perhaps we cannot prove the value of every species, they say, but we must make a "leap of faith." This pulpit rhetoric has become the standard in environmental writing and teaching.[11]

Unfortunately, the priests of the environmental movement have been successful at insinuating their myths and pseudo-science into our schools and universities. This may possibly account for the financial success of their various enterprises. Kaufman finds parallels between modern, environmentalist-inspired education and the catechism.[12] Elementary education in Christian countries not so long ago consisted in large part of learning the catechism by heart and parroting it before the priest or minister. Rote learning of the Koran in Muslim countries is notorious and still much practiced. But the difference between those two and elementary education in what we like to think of as enlightened western countries in the modern age is perhaps less than we would like to think.

Not surprisingly, some churchmen have found a common ground with environmentalists. Both in Norway and the United States, and probably elsewhere as well, they have become engaged in the battle against global warming. This is the modern version of Doomsday and one that is probably easier to get people to believe in than the traditional variety. Computer-based predictions about global warming and extreme weather events are easier to sell to the modern man and woman than stories about virgins giving birth and corpses rising from their graves, ultimately ascending to heaven. Is the church in a transition from the cross to the computer?

A THREAT TO CIVILIZATION?

So we seem to be dealing with an ideology which has some of the characteristics of religion, not in the sense of being otherworldly and relying on supernatural forces, but in making nature herself and her workings sacred and a barrier to human efforts. Just as ideologies such as socialism and the great religions of the world, environmentalism covers a wide area of views and a vast number of people, all of whom may disagree strongly among themselves on many things having to do with the environment, just as the socialists disagree on economic policy and Christians and Muslims on many matters related to their holy books. But just as the ideology of socialism can lead people to go for silly economic policies and the great religions can entice their followers to commit atrocities in the name of their prophets, so environmentalism can encourage irrational policies and even entice their followers to commit sabotage that may lead to manslaughter to safeguard what suits them to call rights of nature. Environmentalism of the ecofundamentalist type is not just a folly which adds color to the gray shades of our daily life (some environmentalist publications are good substitutes for the theater of the absurd), it can be a serious impediment to human progress. In its most extreme variants it is thoroughly anti-human. Listen to this sermon by one of the icons of ecofundamentalism and founder of the Sierra Club, John Muir, addressing alligators: "Honorable representatives of the great saurians of older creation, may you long enjoy your lilies and rushes, and be blessed now and then with a mouthful of terror-stricken man by way of a dainty."[13] I would like to believe that this was said tongue in cheek, but one's sense of humor may speak volumes about one's values and outlook. However that may be, numerous poor fishermen and water-fetching women in Africa are killed every year by crocodiles, a species the protection of which is eagerly sought by urban environmentalists in rich countries. And here is another one, from David M. Graber, a biologist:

> Human happiness, and certainly human fecundity, are not as important as a wild and healthy planet. I know social scientists who remind me that people are part of nature, but it isn't true. Somewhere along the line—at about a billion years ago, maybe half that—we quit the contract and became a cancer. We have become a plague upon ourselves and upon the earth. . . . Until such a time as Homo sapiens should decide to rejoin nature, some of us can only hope for the right virus to come along.[14]

In the light of this it is perhaps superfluous to ask how dangerous environmentalism is as an ideology. George Reisman, after using both of the above quotations, refers to it as "pure, unadulterated poison," expressing "ideas and wishes which, if acted upon, would mean terror and death for enormous numbers of human beings."[15] This may sound intemperate, but the sad thing is that these words are not entirely out of place given the quoted pronouncements and similar ones by other ecofundamentalists. The very least one can say is that environmentalism in its most extreme version is outrightly hostile to economic growth and material well-being. It sees nature as above humanity, to be interfered with as little as possible. A mind-set of this kind could put up barriers against economic development and possibly move developed countries backward. It is indeed the latter that is most likely, as environmentalism has its greatest following in affluent societies. But can ideologies tear down societies? They surely can put them on an unfortunate path, as witnessed by the communist experiments of the twentieth century.

In cases where societies have collapsed they are usually thought to have done so for material reasons such as climate change or development of more powerful enemies that conquered them, but not for reason of a perverse religion or ideology. But there is an interesting discussion ongoing about the collapse of the Mayan civilization, which has a certain relevance in this context. There are two competing theories about the Mayan collapse, one that explains it by an adverse climate change and another that emphasizes the excesses of religion. The first is discussed in Jared Diamond's famous book *Collapse*, but did not originate with him. The thesis is that a drier climate reduced the harvests and thereby the ability of the Mayans to feed themselves. The latter thesis, put forward by Arthur Demarest in his book *Ancient Maya*, holds that the demands of the ceremonial class outgrew the ability of society to support it. As a consequence, wars broke out, and Mayan cities were largely or wholly abandoned. There is no way at this time to tell which is correct, and there could in fact be elements of truth in both; an adverse climate change could have diminished the ability of the ordinary Mayans to support the ceremonial class and made it more aggressive and desperate. In any case the Mayans and their languages survived the alleged collapse.

These two theses illustrate the controversy over the power of ideas versus objective forces in shaping the fate of civilization. Climate change is an objective force with a potential to bring down a civilization. As it ran its course, it may indeed have shaped the ceremonial culture and affected how the climate change played out in Mayan society. By contrast, ascribing the collapse of Mayan society to the demands of its ceremonial class is to give primacy to ideas. Ideas inappropriate in the sense of overburdening the productive activities that support them are thought to be powerful enough on their own to bring a civilization down; for this no climate change would be needed. If we ascribe such power to ideas, it is not far-fetched to imagine environmentalism in its most extreme form as bringing down western civilization. The use of fossil energy and nuclear energy would be abandoned. Hydroelectric power and wind might be tolerated, although by the most extreme environmentalists only reluctantly. Given that less than 10 percent of our primary energy comes from renewable sources and given the pervasive role energy plays in modern society the effect of this on society is simply beyond imagination. But a more likely candidate as an ideology causing a collapse is an excessively cuddly welfare state, sapping the energies of the productive class. It could be compared with the demands of an excessive priesthood.

NOTES

1. Morriss et al. (2011), p. 49, citing the Energy Information Agency.
2. Quoted from Nelson (1991), p. 308.
3. Quoted in Westad (2012), p. 78.
4. See Gibbon (1993/1776–78), Vol. I, chapter 15, especially pp. 548–49.
5. Gibbon (1993/1776–78), Vol. III, p. 169.
6. See Gibbon (1993/1776–78), Vol. II, pp. 271–72.
7. In Introduction to Gibbon (1993/1776–78), Vol. I, p. xcii.
8. Gibbon (1993/1776–1778), Vol. II, p. 548.
9. See, for example, Simon (1999), pp. 107–21, Nelson (2010), and Fitzsimmons (1999), chapter 5.
10. Published in *Three Speeches by Michael Crichton*, Science and Public Policy Institute, December 2009.
11. Kaufman (1994), pp. 7–8.
12. Kaufman (1994), pp. 85–91.
13. Quoted in George Reisman, *The Toxicity of Environmentalism*, Laguna Hills, California: The Jefferson School of Philosophy, Economics and Psychology, 1990, p. 4.
14. *Los Angeles Times Book Review*, October 22, 1989, p. 9.
15. George Reisman, *The Toxicity of Environmentalism*, in *Man and Nature*, The Foundation for Economic Education, Irvington-on-Hudson, New York, 1993, p. 92.

Chapter Three

Sustainability

Lifestyles of the rich . . . are the source of the primary risk to our common future. They are simply not sustainable.

—Maurice Strong, Canadian multimillionaire and first director
of the United Nations Environmental Program.
Quoted in Sheehan (2000), p. 147

[A] sustainable path for the economy is thus not necessarily one that conserves every single thing or any single thing. It is one that replaces whatever it takes from its inherited natural and produced environment, its material and intellectual endowment. What matters is not the particular form that the replacement takes, but only its capacity to produce the things that posterity will enjoy. Those depletions and investment decisions are proper focus.

—Robert Solow, winner of the Nobel Memorial Prize in Economics,
quoted in *Case Western Law Review*, Vol. 53, No. 2, Winter 2002,
Symposium on Bjørn Lomborg's The Skeptical Environmentalist, p. 447

"Sustainability" has become one of the most ubiquitous and meaningless catchphrases of our times. It is natural to begin a discussion of this idea with a discussion of the book *The Limits to Growth*, published in 1972. The book was concerned with the finiteness of natural resources and, more generally, with our economic activities exceeding the carrying capacity of the planet, which sustainability is all about.

The Limits to Growth is a report from a project initiated by the Club of Rome, a club of self-appointed and well heeled sages who felt the world was heading in the wrong direction. The project had an ambitious title, "The Project on the Predicament of Mankind," and its purpose was described in the

21

foreword to the book as "to examine the complex of problems troubling men of all nations: poverty in the midst of plenty; degradation of the environment; loss of faith in institutions; uncontrolled urban spread; insecurity of employment; alienation of youth; rejection of traditional values; and inflation and other monetary and economic disruptions." Global warming is conspicuously absent from the list; this was a time when prominent climate experts believed a new ice age might be imminent. Some items on this list would surely figure on a similar list today, especially if made up by grumpy old men who would surely worry about alienation of youth and rejection of traditional values. Financial crises would replace worries about inflation. The project was paired down to a more manageable study of five critical factors for human survival: population, agricultural production, natural resources, industrial production, and pollution. The study was carried out at the Massachusetts Institute of Technology under the leadership of Jay Forrester, implementing his state of the art methodology to study dynamic systems. The book *The Limits to Growth* summarized the results.

The book was presented, and reviewed, with much hyperbole. On the front cover of the paperback edition it is described as a "headline-making report on the imminent global disaster facing humanity—and what we can do about it before time runs out." Anthony Lewis at the *New York Times* described it as "one of the most important documents of our age!" Then, as we flip the cover, we read the following:

WILL THIS BE THE WORLD THAT YOUR GRANDCHILDREN WILL THANK YOU FOR?

A world where industrial production has sunk to zero. Where population has suffered a catastrophic decline. Where the air, sea, and land are polluted beyond redemption. Where civilization is a distant memory.

This is the world that the computer forecasts. What is even more alarming, the collapse will not come gradually, but with awesome suddenness, with no way of stopping it.

The litany sounds familiar, even if this was written over 40 years ago.

The central theme of the book is what the title suggests, that endless exponential growth is not possible in a finite world. In one sense this is trivial. Obviously there are limits to how many people can be fed from finite land, there is a limit to how much oil or minerals can be dug out, etc. The interesting questions are how far are we from these limits? Are there self-correcting mechanisms that will set in as we approach them? Are these limits set in stone, as it were, or do they depend on our knowledge? On this the book had few answers, and whatever it had has turned out to be wrong, as we shall see. The fundamental contribution of the book was to demonstrate that the combination of exponential growth and delayed adjustment would most likely result in a sudden, catastrophic collapse. A more appropriate but less saleable title would have been "Variations on exponential growth and delay-difference equations."

The analysis behind the book is one of a highly aggregated and simplified system of the world economy, including its population and the ability of the environment to deal with "pollution," that is, various by-products such as pesticides, carbon dioxide, sulfur dioxide, various carcinogens, etc., which would accumulate and harm human health. It showed that exponential growth in population and production would ultimately result in a sudden collapse of both. The model runs had a time horizon up to 2100, but the authors stressed repeatedly that they were not trying to predict accurately the time of collapse, only demonstrate the qualitative behavior of the world economy. Still, they repeatedly made the prediction that the collapse would happen well before the end of the twenty-first century and probably before 2070 (the phrase used on page 29 is "within the next one hundred years").

More than 40 years have gone by and the collapse is still pending. It was predicted to come suddenly and unexpectedly, so we can still hold our breath. But there are few signs of its coming. One such might be the rise in food prices that we have seen recently. These price rises are due to several forces; an increasing world population, an increasing conversion of plant products to the production of biofuels, and a rapid rise in income in some of what used to be the poor countries of the world, China in particular. Interestingly, in many of the model runs collapses due to depletion of minerals or excessive pollution precede and cause the collapse of population. But we are nowhere near running out of minerals and oil, and pollution is not a major problem. Civilization is not yet just a distant memory.

What were the proposed remedies? Unsurprisingly, the authors proposed limiting population growth through birth control and stopping economic growth through limiting investment to needed replacement of capital equipment. Births and deaths can be counted, so the population policy is certainly feasible, but in what kind of society we shall return to shortly. But control of production capital? Economists have scratched their heads, and split hairs, over how to measure the stock of production capital (buildings, infrastructure, machines, etc.). In any case it would require tight economic planning, a process of which we have some experience from the time of the Soviet Union. Do we want to repeat that experiment? And would the countries of the world agree to keeping the capital stock of the world constant? What room would there be for poor countries that need to build up capital in order to escape from poverty? Would the rich countries make room for them by running down their capital stock and forsake their material well-being? Raising these questions says all we need to hear about the feasibility of this remedy.

One country, China, has implemented a strict regime of population growth through its one-child policy. China post-Mao is best characterized as enlightened dictatorship. While such regimes have their advantages they are not likely to be emulated by countries with democratic governments. Besides, dictatorships face a certain risk of sliding into corruption and self-serving behavior (most of them are that way from the beginning). The methods of the one-child policy of China would not get a welcome reception in western democracies that place a higher value on individual rights; in India a sterilization campaign in the 1970s and 1980s ran into fierce opposition and is alleged to have lost Indira Gandhi an election. Here is how Michael Weisskopf, a journalist from the *Washington Post*, describes the one child policy after returning from China:

> [One campaign in Northern China], described by a participating doctor, began in November 1983, when officials from every commune in the county searched their records for women under the age of 45 with two or more children. Then they broadcast their names over public loudspeakers and set dates by which each had to report to the clinic for [sterilization]. There was a warning to potential evaders: the loss of half of their state land allotment, a fine of $200—equal to about a year's income—and a late fee of $10 for every day they failed to report.[1]

There is no doubt that the consequences of unlimited population growth are beyond individual decisions. But there is no doubt either that interfering with those types of decisions gets us beyond current western concepts of individual rights and is likely to require methods such as just described, if not worse. Before applying methods like these, we would do well to consider whether there might be some built-in corrective mechanisms to population growth, in which case we could spare ourselves measures like these. The answer is yes, so it seems, as I shall return to in chapter 7.

Whatever the methods, the one-child policy is likely to have been beneficial for the unprecedented economic growth in China after Mao. Fewer children means fewer mouths to feed, which is important for a poor country, and China is not exactly underpopulated. This policy is likely to have helped the migration from the interior of China to the rapidly developing coastal areas and thus fueled China's economic growth; most of the migrants leave their offspring with their grandparents while away for months or even years at a time. Leaving behind just one child is a lot easier than leaving, say, six, not least on the aging grandparents, and then there is the time otherwise "lost" in pregnancy and nursing several children.

That some underdeveloped economies, China in particular, would begin to grow rapidly and catch up with rich countries was something *The Limits to Growth* certainly did not foresee. It pointed out that economic growth mostly took place in countries that were rich already, with the poor falling further and further behind. It extrapolated a gross national product per capita to year 2000 with China half way between India (above) and Nigeria (below), a figure for Japan twice that for the United States, and a West Germany about half of the United States. But as the book itself put it, these prolongations of trends were not forecasts. That was a wise caveat; they would have been wide off the mark.

As can be seen in the graphs shown in *The Limits to Growth*, some runs of the model used in the study resulted in the world running out of nonrenewable resources some time before 2050, leading to a collapse in industrial production and world population. The resource variable in the model represents an amalgamation of minerals and petroleum, but two important real world categories behind that aggregate are iron and crude oil. If we look at the statistics for these we find that the world has been able to cope with a handsome increase in the use of both; world production of crude steel has increased almost threefold since *The Limits to Growth* was put together, from 575 million tonnes in 1969 to 1,547 million tonnes in 2012. The production of iron ore has risen even more rapidly, from 508 million tonnes in 1980 to 1922 in 2011.[2] As to crude oil, we find that production has almost doubled, from 2,357 million tonnes in 1970 to 4,119 in 2012.[3] But we also see indications of a corrective mechanism that reduces the growth in use of nonrenewable resources as countries grow richer or as prices rise. The production of crude steel in the United Kingdom and the United States has fallen since 1969: in the United Kingdom it was 26 million tonnes in 1969 but 10 in 2012, and in the United States it was 128 million tonnes in 1969 but 89 in 2012. Some of this is undoubtedly due to increased imports of steel products, but it is probably also due to a lower share of steel products in the overall consumption as countries get richer. As to oil, the growth in consumption of crude oil came to an abrupt halt in 1980, after the leap in the oil price in the 1970s; it reached a peak in 1979 at 3,108 million tonnes, a level not surpassed until 1990, and in 2012 it was 4,131 million tonnes. Despite increases in the consumption of oil, proven reserves of oil have hovered around 40 years of consumption for decades. That said, the high price of crude oil since early this century may well be an indication that we are running out of cheap oil. This will temper or reverse the growth in the use of oil, as it did back in the 1980s (see Figure 3.2).

Taking a look at the production of crude steel and crude oil in a long time perspective, we see that there is a certain tendency for the rate of growth to fall over time. Figures 3.1 and 3.2 present the production of steel and oil on logarithmic form, so that a straight line indicates a constant exponential rate of growth. This was largely true for steel from 1900 to 1974, albeit with great

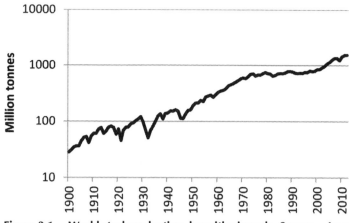

Figure 3.1.   World steel production, logarithmic scale. Source.   Iron and Steel Institute; *Steel Statistical Yearbook.*

variability before the Second World War. It was true for oil from 1945 to 1979. After that the rate of growth fell sharply for both, but for steel it picked up again around 2000 as a result of the rapid growth in China and other underdeveloped countries. I shall return to oil in chapter 5.

We can take it for granted that there is a limit to how many people can be supported by the ability of the planet to supply food. But we do not know exactly where that limit is, and it has moved outwards due to increases in productivity. We also know there is a limit to how much minerals and petroleum we can extract, but we have little idea where that limit is. What lesson are we supposed to draw from this? That we should immediately take steps

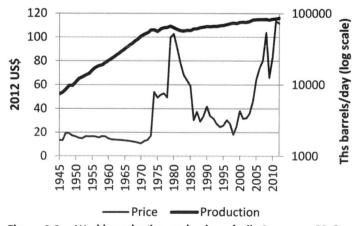

Figure 3.2.   World production and price of oil. Sources. *BP Statistical Review of World Energy* **and Statistics Norway:** *Oil and Gas Yearbook 1986.*

to stop and perhaps reverse economic growth and population growth? That seems to be the prescription of *The Limits to Growth*; on page 157 we read the following (italics in the original): *"Is it better to try to live within that limit by accepting a self-imposed restriction on growth? Or is it preferable to go on growing until some other natural limit arises, in the hope that at that time another technological leap will allow growth to continue still longer?"* Well, the latter is exactly what mankind has been doing, not just since the industrial revolution but throughout its history. We have been trying to improve our lot, we have tried to overcome limits, more often than not successfully. This is our recipe for progress. One may wonder what the world would look like today if in 1975 we would have made the leap for zero economic growth. We did not, and the end is not yet in sight, civilization is not yet a distant memory.

SUSTAINABLE DEVELOPMENT

Despite its simplicity and wrongheadedness, *The Limits to Growth* was influential. Its predictions were dire, and, as we have seen, it recommended an end to economic growth without reservation. But the divide between rich and poor nations was glaring, and most countries had economic development on their agenda, even rich countries, which donated money to poor countries as development aid. Would it be possible to accomplish economic development and still keep within the confines set by the limited carrying capacity of the planet? To investigate this, the UN set up the World Commission on Environment and Development. The commission delivered its report, *Our Common Future*, in 1987 and launched the concept "sustainable development," defined as a process that "meets the needs of the present without compromising the ability of future generations to meet their own needs." A nice idea, but what does it mean? Over the years sustainable development has become a ubiquitous phrase used for all things great and good, often apparently without much thought. Hordes of academics have labored on clarifying the concept, without accomplishing a great deal.

As is abundantly clear from *Our Common Future*, the idea of sustainable development arose from two concerns. First, there was the notion that the world was depleting its resources, both renewable and nonrenewable ones. This is where the sustainability part comes from. Second, there was the enormous discrepancy between rich and poor in the world. This is where the development part comes from. But lifting billions of people out of poverty requires enormous increase in use of resources, so solving the second problem would appear to aggravate the first. The notion of sustainable development was the commission's way of squaring the circle.

The report says preciously little, however, about how exactly this is to be done; it is short on specifics but long on wishful thinking. Despite *Our Common Future* and the deluge that has been written on sustainable development since its appearance, development is still as unsustainable as ever. No single country in the world has made greater gains in economic development since *Our Common Future* was written than China. The development of China has been just as much characterized by increased reliance on nonrenewable natural resources as the industrial revolution in the western world in its day. China has become the largest oil importing country in the world, and its imports of iron and coal have multiplied several times over. For a while, China was reported as opening a new coal fired power station every week. The rapid industrialization of China and the associated rise in living standards are widely admired and something other poor countries of the world seek to emulate. Similar developments have indeed taken place elsewhere, albeit on a smaller scale, such as in Vietnam and Brazil. But it has not been in harmony with the message of *Our Common Future*. The deliberations and efforts going into that report apparently were just a waste of time. Reading it now, a quarter of a century after its publication, the most striking thing is how irrelevant it has been for all that has happened in the meantime.

Not everyone would agree with this. The authors of the book *Cents and Sustainability*, a 400-page panegyric on *Our Common Future*, argue that the link between economic growth and the use of resources has been broken.[4] They show examples of economic growth occurring in selected countries without much increase in the use of energy and even despite a decline. But their examples are all taken from rich countries. The picture that emerges when we also consider poor and medium rich countries is quite different. Figure 3.3 shows the annualized growth rates of energy use and gross domestic product (GDP) in 17 of the world's most populous countries.[5] The periods are chosen with a view to the development in the price of oil (see Figure 3.2). The period 1950–1973 was one of a stable and slightly falling real price of oil. Then came the quadrupling of the oil price in 1973–1974 and a further doubling in 1979–1980. In 1986 the oil price fell precipitously and stayed relatively low until 2004–2005. Since 2004 the price of oil (Brent) has risen to unprecedented heights; from about $40 to more than $100, but with major gyrations.

What we see in Figure 3.3 is that the growth in energy use has in most cases been about as high or higher than the growth in GDP. This has been the case in China, India, Indonesia, Brazil, Mexico, Turkey, Thailand, Iran, South Africa, Egypt, the Philippines, and South Korea. All these countries are poor or medium rich. Most of them have been growing fast, and some would now be characterized as rich (South Korea, for example). They all are in, or have been through, a phase of industrialization where the economic

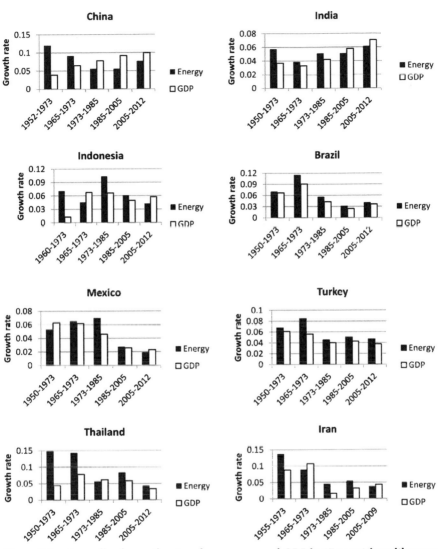

Figure 3.3. Annualized growth rates of energy use and GDP in 17 countries with more that 50 million inhabitants. Source: See main text.

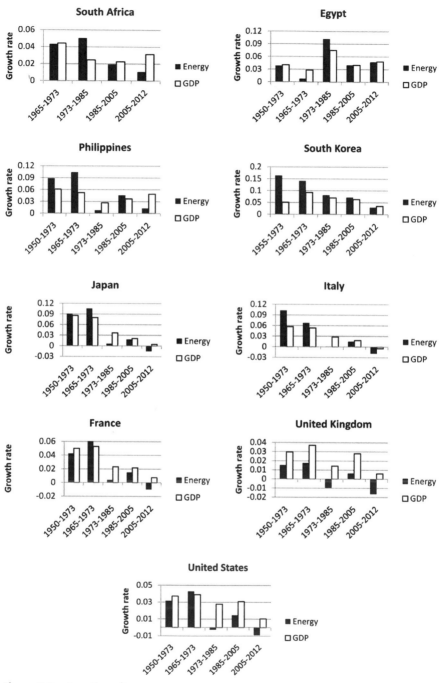

Figure 3.3. (*continued*)

growth is strongly correlated with growth in the use of energy. China is in fact somewhat exceptional in that energy use has grown more slowly than GDP since its economic development took off in the 1980s, but the growth rates of both have been high. Also the Philippines are a bit special in that the growth in energy use has been slow in periods of high oil prices, but the Philippines are not a paragon of economic development. We also see much of the same pattern in some of the rich countries. Japan and Italy went through a phase of rapid growth in the 1950s and 1960s, and the growth in energy use was higher than the growth of GDP in this period. For the other rich countries (France, the United Kingdom, the United States), we see a much lower rate of growth in energy use than in GDP after 1972 (for the United Kingdom this has been so ever since 1950). It is also in these countries that we see sensitivity to the oil price; the use of energy grew much less than GDP, or even declined, in the periods of high oil price (1973–1985 and after 2004). We see much less of that in the poor countries, except the Philippines.

So here we have the "decoupling" between economic growth and energy use, touted in *Cents and Sustainability*. It is a rich country phenomenon and occurring in response to higher oil prices. One thing can be added to this. The decline in energy use in rich countries, at least in relative terms, has also been caused by the "outsourcing" of energy intensive production to China and other rapidly developing countries. In his book *The Carbon Crunch*, Dieter Helm refers to an investigation he made of the carbon dioxide emissions in the United Kingdom, calculated on the basis of consumption rather than production. He found that the emissions have increased about as much since 1990 if we look at consumption as they have declined if we look at production. It is not obvious that we should base our accounting and blame game on production rather than consumption; the reason we do so is that it is so much simpler to assess the emissions on the basis of production.

Returning to the question of sustainability, we should not be surprised that the notion of sustainable development does not get us very far. As far as nonrenewable resources are concerned it does not get us anywhere. Exploiting a nonrenewable resource is by definition not sustainable; a barrel of oil extracted today will not be available tomorrow, and ultimately all the extractable oil will be gone. The fact that the total extractable reserves have an economic dimension does not fundamentally alter that fact; it only makes the total amount more fuzzy, but it does not make it infinite. The interesting questions we can ask in this context are how long will the resources last and will it be possible to replace them. We do not know the answers to either question, but if experience is any guide we will probably do just fine.

Whether or not we will be able to replace nonrenewable fuels and minerals with energy and materials from renewable sources is a question of technological development. Technological development is unpredictable and goes beyond our imagination. It is well illustrated by a passage in Stanley Jevons' book *The Coal Question*: ". . . even if an aërial machine could be propelled by some internal power from 50 to a 100 miles per hour it could not make head against a gale." This was written 40 years before the flight of the Wright brothers so we should not berate Jevons for a lack of foresight; he was one of the most outstanding English economists of his time, and we who live in the early twenty-first century are undoubtedly equally limited in our ability to predict the future.

The technological development that has taken place within our lifetime and that of our parents and grandparents gives reasons for optimism. We do have wind power, solar power, and nuclear power, even if the first two are currently uncompetitive with fossil fuels and the last is not renewable, but fissile material is fairly abundant. But even if we, for the sake of the argument, accept that nonrenewable resources are truly irreplaceable, that there never will be any substitutes on a sufficient scale for fossil fuels and for minerals, should we automatically conclude that the industrial revolution should never have happened? If this were true, we would have the choice, in Jevons' words, "between true greatness and a long, drawn-out mediocrity." Now that we have discovered the use of minerals and fossil fuels we could do as the fabled Irish farmer who knew there was peat in his land. He realized that the peat could not last forever. Concerned as he was with just distribution among generations, or as just as circumstances would allow, he estimated how much peat was in his land, figured out how much peat each generation would need just to survive, made a vow not to dig up more than his just share, and made his son make a similar vow. So it went on for a few generations until no more peat was dug up, not because all the peat was gone but because the need for it had disappeared; new and more convenient fuels had come on the scene.

Looking back on the human achievements since the industrial revolution it seems well worth having, even if it were to turn out unsustainable. Environmentalists who take pride in predicting doom and gloom are doing so from the comforts produced by the industrial revolution and would not be doing so without it. It seems a doubtful proposition to go back to pre-industrial times. Apart from the fact that such policies would hardly be made voluntarily, it is also possible to argue that our current and in simplistic terms unsustainable way of life might in fact be the only feasible way of giving some meaning to the worn cliché of sustainable development. Economic growth, technological development, and the use of energy are strongly interrelated, as we have seen. It is quite possible that the advancements in technology that make it possible for us to extract ever more of nonrenewable resources in ever more challenging locations will also place us in a better position to move away from fossil fuels and minerals when and to the extent we need to. We might thus be faced with the paradox that the more prolific we are in our use of resources today, the better placed we will be to do without them tomorrow. This might in fact be the only sensible kind of sustainable development we could engage in. Any use of nonrenewable resources is by definition not sustainable, if by sustainable development we mean a process that repeats itself over time in an identical fashion. But human progress is not like that. The only sustainable development we can meaningfully engage in is leaving a technologically more advanced world to our children than the one we inherited, to make them better able to face the challenges they in turn will be faced with. Perhaps the least sensible thing we can do is to bequeath to our children endowments for use decades down the road and which appear useful given the current state of technology. What would our grandparents have done if they had wanted to promote our well-being rather than their own? Would they have been prolific in building roads for horses and carts and other infrastructure for their own technology? About a hundred years ago there were concerns that ash trees, good for making skis, would become scarce in Norway, and ash trees were duly planted for future ski making. To little avail. Nowadays skis are made of synthetic material. Last time a world record was set on wooden skis was in 1970.

Although at one level it is easy to understand how the concerns about sustainable development came about, at another it is odd. For what do we see other than progress as we look back on human history? It has not been uninterrupted, and it has evolved unevenly; it is sometimes said that Europe slid backwards from the fall of Rome until the Renaissance, a period of a thousand years. Yet, which generation of our forefathers would we want to change places with? The answer to that question tells us something about human progress. That progress was certainly not based on the notion of sustainable development, and the greatest leap in that progress, the industrial revolution, was based on a patently unsustainable use of fossil fuels.

Hence, if sustainable development means anything it cannot be a process that repeats itself over and over again in an immutable fashion, it must be a process that constantly changes as our knowledge and technology changes and leads to an improved standard of living, albeit in the long run and by occasional setbacks and leaps. There is no way in which we can leave behind a world as rich in nonrenewable resources as the one we inherited other than not use them at all. But that would be a miserable world. Our use of resources maintains a civilization that has shown itself able to maintain itself at a rising standard of living. Our use of resources has not just fueled enjoyment, it has also maintained an expanding base of science and technology that has enabled us to overcome the problems we have encountered. The ultimate irony is that economic growth became sustained after the industrial revolution when we began to rely on nonrenewable energy sources.[6] Will it also be sustainable? Possibly and probably, in the sense of Solow, quoted at the beginning of this chapter.

SUSTAINABILITY AND RENEWABLE RESOURCES

For living resources, such as forests, plants, animals, and fish, sustainable use is clearly possible, as these resources grow naturally, although with major fluctuations. But even here it is unclear that sustainable development in the sense of a repetitive, unchanging process is what we want. Let us take fish as an example. An unexploited fish stock may be thought of as being in a natural equilibrium, with annual growth being matched by annual decay. Fishing reduces the stock, but that in turn generates surplus growth, and if we limit our fishing to the surplus growth the stock could be maintained indefinitely. Many fish stocks have been exploited since time immemorial without going extinct, confirming this hypothesis. We can think of the relationship between the size of a fish stock and its surplus growth as the dome-shaped curve in Figure 3.4. A stock in natural equilibrium produces no surplus growth, and neither does a stock that has been totally depleted (or depleted below the minimum viable level). In between there will be some surplus growth that we can utilize sustainably. We may also note that a sustainable exploitation of a fish stock implies that we reduce it below its natural equilibrium level; there is no way that we can preserve a pristine stock and exploit it at the same time.

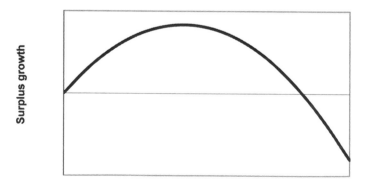

Figure 3.4. Surplus growth of a fish stock as a function of stock size.

But which level should we select? We see that there are many sustainable stock levels and associated surplus growth rates. Sustainability alone does not tell us which one to choose. Would not maximum sustainable yield (surplus growth) be the thing to go for? Well, that would mean applying one more criterion than sustainability alone. And what about the costs of fishing? Note that any given level of sustainable yield, except the maximum, can be taken from two different stock levels. Would fishing costs not modify our choice if it is cheaper to fish from a large stock than from a small one? Yes, they would. And what about time discounting? Might it be permissible to catch an unsustainable amount of fish for some time and reduce the stock below the level that maximizes sustainable yield and so sacrifice some sustainable catches of fish for a temporary gain? Yes, it might. So, to select the right sustainable long term strategy we must go beyond the concept of sustainability itself.

But the problems really begin when we consider natural variability. Growth and regeneration of fish stocks are strongly affected by natural conditions over which we have little or no control. This is related to supplies of nutrition; small fish need zooplankton of the right kind and at the right time to survive, older and bigger fish need feed in the form of smaller prey fish to grow and maintain themselves. The supply of both of these varies enormously from year to year for reasons that are not at all well known, but are often proxied by fluctuations in ocean currents manifesting themselves in variations of ocean temperature or salinity. Sustainable use of fish stocks must be implemented within these constraints and with a view toward the future, about which there is much uncertainty. Sustainable fishing is not likely to mean an even catch of fish over time; fish stocks must be managed with a view toward the environmental conditions in the ocean at each time and how they are expected to develop. In most cases this is likely to mean fish catches that fluctuate from year to year, even if they are perfectly sustainable in the long term. We shall see examples of this in chapter 8.

And then we come to the question whether it is at all desirable to exploit renewable resources on a sustainable basis. Should we cut down a forest once and for all and never plant it again, or should we replace it with seedlings which we in turn can cut down as they have grown into suitably big trees? Over time man has cut down innumerable forests in order to make place for his cities and the farms where he grows his food. Currently there is much discussion about preserving the rain forests of the Amazon and Southeast Asia. Well, that is not what our ancestors did with much of their forests. Some forests we certainly need, but how much and where? The idea of sustainable development does not get us much closer to answering that question. Today's environmentalists lament the loss of biodiversity and proliferation of alien species due to the loss of land to our cities and farms. Fortunately for us, including the environmentalists themselves, preservation of biodiversity and fight against alien species are of a recent vintage.

There are further problems. What is it that we want to sustain? Is it good enough to replace the trees we cut down with new ones? Much controversy has sprung up about so-called old growth forests. Some environmentalists want to preserve forests in their pristine state and let them regenerate in a natural way instead of cutting them down, replacing the trees we take with seedlings. Sometimes this is motivated by pristine forests supporting wildlife which would die out if large areas were laid waste and planted with seedlings. This comes pretty close to declaring areas and their wildlife sacred and untouchable, much as the superstitious religions of primitive huntsmen did for certain places in times past. And that analogy is not far-fetched; as a matter of fact, some environmentalists invoke the alleged wisdom of primitive huntsmen in the past as an argument for leaving nature alone.

THE PRECAUTIONARY PRINCIPLE

Related to sustainability is the so-called precautionary principle. This is a good illustration of the backward-looking and conservative nature of environmentalism. It is frequently invoked when environmentalists want to prevent something they perceive as harmful for the environment. What kind of a principle is this? Or, more to the point, is it a principle at all?

The precautionary principle is about placing the burden of proof. What do we do if a product or an activity is potentially harmful for the environment? Do we ban it or do we allow it? Given that there is uncertainty about the outcome, the answer is largely given by placing the burden of proof. Is it necessary to prove that the product or activity is harmless for the environment? In that case the product or activity will be banned before it even got started. But if harmful effects have to be demonstrated for a ban to be put in place, uncertainty about the outcome would mean that there would be no ban until after the product or activity had been introduced and proven to be dangerous.

Not surprisingly, environmentalists have advocated the precautionary principle. This makes it possible for them to prevent all sorts of products and activities which they perceive as potentially harmful, even if there is no evidence and little presumption that they are. But how sensible is this? Should this "principle" be applied even on the flimsiest of indications that the activity or product could be harmful? Many have balked at this, which has led to a watered-down version of the precautionary principle. In fact the version in the declaration from the environmental summit in Rio de Janeiro in 1992 can be so characterized. Rather than using the term "precautionary principle" it talks about "precautionary approach" and states that "[W]here there are threats of serious or irreversible damage, lack of full scientific certainty shall not be used as a reason for postponing cost-effective measures to prevent environmental degradation." Obviously, this implies some judgment of how important the environmental risk is, which is certainly the common sense approach and hardly a principle. Environmentalists would, on the other hand, prefer a more absolutist version, what has come to be known as the strong version of the precautionary principle. One version, formulated at a meeting in 1998 (The Wingspread Conference on the Precautionary Principle, convened by the Science and Environmental Health Network) has it like this: "When an activity raises threats of harm to human health or the environment, precautionary measures should be taken even if some cause and effect relationships are not fully established scientifically." Note that nothing is said about how severe the threat is or the importance of the benefits the activity would bring.

In fact, adhering to the precautionary principle involves more than just placing the burden of proof. There is, needless to say, little or no evidence supporting hypothetical dangers of products or projects. Environmentalists are known for making bold and even outlandish claims about these. The Brent Spar episode mentioned in chapter 8 is a case in point. What limits the claims that environmentalists can make in order to invoke the precautionary principle? Maybe fantasy alone. As a spokesman for a planned copper mine in Alaska (the Pebble mine) has put it: "The opposition is unaccountable for what they say. The industry is held accountable." The Pebble mine is located in Bristol Bay, home to prodigious salmon runs and indigenous tribes. If imagination is the only limit, the effects of this mine could be devastating. How many copper or for that matter other mines in the world would have been opened on an absolutist interpretation of the precautionary principle and unlimited powers of the imagination with respect to potential damages?

An uncritical application of the absolutist version of the precautionary principle would be a serious threat for human progress. Think of medical advances, for example. What was known about the effects of vaccines when they were first applied? Indeed there are quite a few people who believe that vaccines are dangerous and refuse to apply them to their children. A case in point is the triple vaccine (mumps, measles, and rubella) alleged to cause autism. This belief may have been caused, and was in any case strengthened, by a research paper in a prestigious scientific journal that was later exposed as fraud.[7] With few or no exceptions the benefits of vaccines are undisputed, even if they may have some harmful side effects. The precautionary principle would have them banned. What about the use of antibiotics? They are not entirely without problems, and the existence of these and more could probably have been imagined when antibiotics first came into use. By banning them at the outset we would have forgone the saving of millions of lives. A deep ecologist might retort that there are too many of us as things are.

Not only would an uncritical application of the absolutist version of the precautionary principle be inimical to progress in the sense of depriving us of useful products, it would deprive us of a source of learning. Among the things we learn from are our mistakes. And the only way to learn about the dangers of a product is by using it. Banning products from the outset is the surest way that we will never learn anything about them. Not for nothing has the precautionary principle been called the paralyzing principle. But of course, if the a priori risk is too high we would never take it. We would not want a short and local nuclear war to play out just to learn about the effects; that it might happen inadvertently is another issue. So a sensible application of the precautionary principle boils down to little more than old-fashioned common sense. The high-flying garb of the Rio Declaration makes little difference in that respect.

But the precautionary principle may have done quite a bit of damage. It has been a convenient rallying cry and lent legitimacy to policies which do not seem to be well taken. It has been invoked by the European Union in its ban of genetically engineered food products. The well fed Europeans can easily afford to forego the productivity gains that genetically engineered food makes possible, but things look less rosy for the billions in the poor and not so rich countries of the world where many are still undernourished and the challenge to feed a growing population is growing day by day. Such countries have typically received genetically engineered seeds with enthusiasm. The parallel to what happened in India as a consequence of the green revolution is striking. Back in the 1960s, India was a basket case of a country with a grain shortage and one that many thought could never feed itself. Then came the green revolution, and grain production in India increased to such an extent that it became self-sufficient and could export grain in good years. Nevertheless, there were those who doubted the blessings of the green revolution; one of the arguments was that it would enrich the few and impoverish the masses.[8] The precautionary principle would have been a good argument to invoke for those who for other reasons wanted to stop the green revolution in its tracks. Fortunately, perhaps, this "principle" surfaced decades later. I shall return to the green revolution in chapter 7.

What if our stone age forefathers had applied the precautionary principle? A myth has it like this. In the late evening, a stone age woman says: "Stop honing that flintstone, dear, you never know where it might end."

And a contemporary example, due to Lester Brown, earlier an enthusiast for the green revolution:

"We are crossing natural thresholds that we cannot see and violating deadlines that we cannot recognize. Nature is the time keeper, but we cannot control the clock."[9]

Really? How did he come to know? Except for the reference to the clock, a device that had not yet been invented, this could have come from the Book of Revelations.

NOTES

1. Quoted by Karl Zinsmeister in Huggins and Skandera (eds., 2004), p. 375.

2. Source: Iron and Steel Institute; *Steel Statistical Yearbook*.

3. Source: *BP Statistical Review of World Energy*.

4. Smith et al. (2010).

5. All these countries have a population of 50 million or more. Countries which have either split or merged (Germany, Russia, Pakistan, Bangladesh, Ethiopia, Vietnam) since 1950 have been left out. Also left out are Nigeria and Congo/Zaire, because they are not explicitly listed in the *BP Statistical Review of World Energy*. The sources are as follows. Energy use: *UN Yearbook of Energy Statistics* (1950–1965); *BP Statistical Review of World Energy* (1965–2011). GDP: *Penn World Table* (1950–1965); index for real GDP per capita multiplied by population; World Bank (1965–2012); GDP in 2005 US$. From this the annualized growth rates for the selected periods have been calculated.

6. See Ridley (2010), pp. 216–17 and p. 231.

7. See articles by B. Deer and F. Godlee, J. Smith and H. Marcovitch in the *British Medical Journal*, 2011.

8. See, for example, (Griffin, 1979).

9. Lester Brown (2008).

Chapter Four

Biodiversity, Alien Species, and "Iconic" Animals

Lóan heim úr lofti flaug
(ljómaði sól um himinbaug
blómi grær á grundu)
til að annast unga smá
alla étið hafði þá
hrafn fyrir hálfri stundu.

[The bird flew back to her nest
(Sunshine all around
Flowers blooming below)
To feed her little chicks
Raven had eaten them all
Half an hour ago]

—Jónas Hallgrímsson, Icelandic, romantic poet (1836)

in the first ages of society, when the fiercer animals often dispute with man the possession of an unsettled country, a successful war against those savages is one of the most innocent and beneficial labours of heroism.

—Edward Gibbon (1993/1776), Vol. I, p. 105

Who has not heard about the need to preserve biodiversity and fight alien species? Or to preserve the health of ecosystems? There is a UN Convention on Biodiversity, put together at the Rio Summit in 1992 and subsequently ratified by more than 30 countries, the necessary minimum for it to enter into force. Its objectives are "the conservation of biological diversity, the sustainable use of its components and the fair and equitable sharing of the benefits . . ." (Article 1). In its wake there has been a deluge of studies monitoring biodiversity and health of ecosystems.

What is all this about? What precisely is biodiversity? Why is it worth preserving? Biodiversity, loosely speaking, must mean a greater variety, either a greater variety of species or greater variety within species. This is also how the Biodiversity Convention defines it (Article 2):

> "Biological diversity" means the variability among living organisms from all sources including, inter alia, terrestrial, marine and other aquatic ecosystems and the ecological complexes of which they are part: this includes diversity within species, between species and of ecosystems.

But even biodiversity must have its limits. There cannot be an infinite number of species on the planet, and there is a limit to the variability within a species; indeed, when the genetic variability gets too great, we have a new species. What, then, could set the limit to the number of species? Ignore for the moment the role of humans and consider a "world without us." Existence is a struggle for life; one species preys upon another, and each tries as best it can to survive. The limit is then determined by which species survive and which not. Over time species have become extinct because not enough individuals could survive, and new species have emerged and evolved through mutations and natural selection. The ecosystem has undergone disturbances, large and small, on various time scales, and so evolved under its own autonomy. Creationists supposedly have a problem with this; why didn't the omniscient creator make a perfect system to begin with? Or is he just experimenting? If so, he would not be omniscient. Do we see a development toward greater perfection? Under this development, and long before humans came on the scene, species became extinct and new ones emerged without any human influence whatever.

How does the existence of humans change this? What distinguishes man is his intelligence and ability to make tools and to communicate and organize; we have learned the laws of nature and turned them to our own advantage. In the sense of maximizing the rate of our own survival it is not fundamentally different from what other animals do; they outcompete their competitors and get rid of them as best they can, but are unable to grow the plants or breed the animals they eat. They probably have no notion of "sustainable" predation or grazing in order to ensure their continued existence; which species survive and which die out is the result of an unfettered and myopic competition. But humans are much better than other animals at ensuring their survival and have therefore outgrown what deep ecologists would call their appropriate place in nature.

It is now roughly ten thousand years since humans began to experiment with agriculture, in China and the Fertile Crescent of the Middle East. What did they do? They sowed plants that once grew in the wild, they bred them selectively to make sure they survived and thrived better. But first they tilled the land and got rid of the plants that were there from before. They were happy enough to keep the worms in the soil, the bacteria and much else, which in the modern lingo provide the necessary "ecosystem services," and the bacteria they would not in any case have known about. But they would have been happy to kill the locusts when they arrived and other parasites that threatened their crops. This was made possible much later by modern science.

Later we have seen this story being repeated on a massive scale in various parts of the world. The North American prairies, once the domain of the buffalo, have long since become the breadbasket not just of the United States and Canada, but much of the rest of the world as well. For this it was necessary to first get rid of the buffalo. In the arid west, the buffalo was replaced by cattle, which are much more convenient producers of meat. Nevertheless, there are quite a few environmentalists who are looking forward to the day when the prairies have been reconquered by the buffalo.

There are many other success stories. Wool and mutton used to be major export articles from Australia and New Zealand. They are still exported from these countries, having been eclipsed by other goods over the years. But the sheep is not indigenous to Australia and New Zealand, and neither are the dairy cows, which also provide a substantial part of New Zealand's exports, and neither are the grapes which make it possible for the Kiwis and the Aussies to produce excellent wines. In truth, the fauna and flora of New Zealand and Australia have been altered beyond recognition by the Europeans who settled there. Less conspicuously, insects and microorganisms have been imported to control pests and weeds in various parts of the world.[1]

Many of us associate coffee with Brazil, which is by far the greatest producer of coffee in the world. But coffee is not indigenous to Brazil. It comes from Ethiopia and turned out to grow well in certain parts of Brazil. Neither is tea indigenous to India and Sri Lanka; the British managed to steal it from China, and it grew well in its new places. And the potato is not indigenous to Ireland, as someone who has heard about the Irish potato famine might think. It comes from the highlands of South America and turned out to be extremely versatile and able to grow in not so benign climes like damp and cool Ireland and sub-Arctic Iceland. In these countries and in Scandinavia and many other places it became a staple over the years and probably saved millions from famine; it was a disease killing the potato that caused the potato famine in Ireland, which had become critically dependent on the potato crop.

Another plant the British got hold of and planted in their empire with great success was the rubber tree. It is indigenous to the Amazon, and the Brazilian city of Manaus was built on the rubber wealth that the Brazilians thought they could have all for themselves. But the British brought it to Malaya, at the time a British colony, so they could have access to their own rubber. It also turned out to thrive in the Dutch East Indies, now known as Indonesia.

So much for alien species and the loss in biodiversity implicit in plantations with monocultures, be it corn or wheat or oil palms or rubber. The world would quite simply be a poorer place without them, and we would probably not be able to feed ourselves. But lately the transplant of successful and useful species has become suspect, despite the usefulness and superiority of the new species over the indigenous ones. In the 1960s the Russians transplanted king crab from the Bering Sea to the Barents Sea. The king crab conquers competing species, but it is a highly valuable one because of its size and delicious taste. It has now spread along the northern part of the Norwegian coast and is caught occasionally by Norwegian fishermen. Probably because of environmentalist influence the king crab is considered unwelcome by the Norwegian authorities who would rather see it disappear than take advantage of it as a source of food and export income.

Another example of a successful but controversial transplant is the Nile perch, which was set out in Lake Victoria in the 1960s. It has pushed aside its competitor, the dagga, a small and bony fish that is much inferior to the fleshy perch. A part of the controversy is that much of the Nile perch is exported while the dagga is consumed by the indigenous population around the lake. But it is not an ecological problem that wealthy Europeans can outbid poor Tanzanians for the Nile perch, and it is doubtful if Tanzania would be better off by foregoing the export revenue from the Nile perch. Yet another successful transplant is the kapenta, a small fish that was set out in the Cabora Bassa dam on the Zambezi River. The kapenta is now an important source of food both in Zambia and in Zimbabwe. It is not suitable for export and so has not been controversial as the Nile perch has been.

Would the advocates of biodiversity rather have us go without these things? Some apparently would. We can find pronouncements such as the following: "To give a sense of the scale of environmental deterioration that has taken place, the MEA (Millennium Ecosystem Assessment) notes that more land has been converted to agriculture since 1945 than in the eighteenth and nineteenth century combined."[2] In the same vein: "The biggest change to ecosystem structure has been the transformation of nearly a quarter of the Earth's terrestrial surface to cultivated systems. Since 1945, 680 million hectares out of 3.5 billion hectares of rangelands have been affected."[3] What a terrible thing. How are the billions of people that have been added to the world population supposed to subsist otherwise? Some environmentalists would say they should not be here in the first place, but getting them out of the way is another matter, and no less so is preventing more of them from being born.

HOW USEFUL IS BIODIVERSITY?

Not infrequently, biodiversity is dressed in the garb that this is useful for us, that it provides "ecosystem services," a phrase drawn from business lingo that has become popular among environmentalists, probably in the expectation that this will enhance the appeal of environmentalism to decision makers and those with money to give away. As pointed out by geographer Allan Fitzsimmons, the metaphor of "ecosystem services" is badly mistaken.[4] Whatever "services" bacteria, worms, and other living things might yield is purely a coincidence of their struggle for their own existence; it just so happens that some of this is useful for us humans. The notion of "service" is from the vantage point of humans; it is as "anthropocentric" as anything could ever be. That irony is probably lost on those who peddle the notion of ecosystem services.

No one would dispute that we need a healthy enough environment to raise our domesticated animals and to grow our food, but quite often that entails eradication of weeds, disease-carrying bacteria and viruses, and predators. Sometimes living things in our environment do us a great "disservice." And we try as best we can to eradicate bacteria or viruses that carry deadly diseases such as polio, malaria, and smallpox. We shower, soap, and shampoo with relish despite its deadly effects on lice and fleas, which traditionally have been our fellow travelers, and I for one am not looking forward to meeting those who do what it takes to ensure their continued existence. Even environmentalists would presumably agree that biodiversity is not good in all its dimensions.

Much has been made of the fact that the new strains of rice and wheat involved in the green revolution were bred from crossing cultivated plant varieties with wild ones. With universal monocultures these wild varieties would not have existed. Similarly, new medicines have been developed from wild plants. So a world without wild plants would have been a world of fewer possibilities. But how many wild plants do we need? Without our massive monocultures we can forget about feeding all seven billion of us, let alone more. Presumably there is a trade-off between cultivation and wilderness, and expansion of the former is not necessarily to be lamented, given our still growing number.

Much of the preservation of biodiversity does not at all concern animals useful for humans, but rather animals that are dangerous to humans or our domesticated animals. A recurrent theme in Norwegian political debate is protection of bears and wolves whose supporters invoke the notion of biodiversity. Sheep and reindeer farmers are of a different opinion; every year thousands of lambs and reindeer calves are slaughtered by bears and wolves and other predators in a way that animal rightists would find abhorrent if it happened in the abattoir. Bear and wolf lovers are found in urban areas where the risk of encountering these animals is nonexistent, but people living in rural areas are less happy about having their children wait for the school bus where they might be attacked by them. In earlier times, farmers tried to kill off these animals as best they could and succeeded to eradicate them in some countries, but in others not. People in countries free of bears and wolves seem to have done just fine in the absence of their "ecosystem services."

Other European countries have similar problems. In recent years the wolves have made a come back in the French Alps.[5] Being a nuisance for sheep raising, the wolf was hunted to extinction in the 1930s. Late last century the European Union made the wolf a protected species, and it invaded the French Alps from Italy in 1992. Since then the wolf population there has multiplied many times over and is now believed to be growing at an annual rate of 20 percent. This is in no small way due to the availability of prey in the form of sheep being grazed in the Alps—20,000 sheep are believed to have been killed by wolves in just five years, according to official counts. And official counts are indeed kept with some care; the French sheep rangers are entitled to damages due to these predations; 90 euros per lamb and 160 euros per ewe, plus a "stress bonus" for the cruel killings. So the wolf is dining at the expense of the French taxpayer. Nevertheless, European Union officials consider the wolf story one of success, but the sheep farmers are less thrilled; even with the said compensation they still lose economically. But the environmentalists face a dilemma. Much as they may like the wild wolves, they also are likely to admire the small scale, "sustainable" farming by way of sheep-grazing; those who buy into local provision of food as a way to save the world may have to make the uncomfortable choice between the sheep and the wolves. It is likely not be as easily resolved as the old riddle of how to ferry a wolf, a lamb, and a bale of hay in a boat with space for only one at a time across a river.

Not infrequently the biodiversity debate follows the end-is-near syndrome. We are told that tens and possibly hundreds of thousands of species are disappearing every year and that in so many years they will all be gone. Both assertions are a bit strange, given that nobody knows how many species there are on the planet to begin with. On top of that, even the definition of what "a species" is and what is not can be problematic.[6] Contrary to what some people may believe, the species that allegedly are going extinct are lowly creatures like insects and not the charismatic megafauna. Relevant or not, the numbers of species allegedly going extinct every year is faith-based rather than fact-based.[7] About a thousand species have been documented as having become extinct since 1600, which, because of required documentary evidence, is likely to be an underestimate. Among these are about a hundred mammals and birds each, and about 80 fish.[8]

How much biodiversity we need and of what kind is not a question with an easy answer, and in any case a deeply "anthropocentric" one. David Ehrenfeld, professor of philosophy, specializing in environmental ethics, puts it this way:

> We do not know how many species [of plants] are needed to keep the planet green, but it seems unlikely to be anywhere near the more than quarter of a million we have now. Even a mighty dominant like the American chestnut, extending over half a continent, all but disappeared without bringing the eastern deciduous forest down with it. And if we turn to the invertebrates, the source of nearly all biological diversity, what biologist is willing to find a value—conventional or ecological—for all 600,000 species of beetles? In short, the ones most likely to become extinct are obviously the ones least likely to be missed by the biosphere. Many of these species were never common or ecologically influential; by no stretch of the imagination can we make them vital cogs in the ecological machine"[9]

VALUING ECOSYSTEM SERVICES

Not surprisingly, the notion of ecosystem services has given rise to attempts to put a value on them. One such was undertaken by Robert Constanza and others in the 1990s.[10] Their list of services is comprehensive enough to encompass all conceivable services, from soil formation and water purification to recreational and cultural activities. The motivation is that these services are not traded in any markets anywhere and therefore prone to be ignored in decisions based on economic or commercial values. Because these services are not traded anywhere their value must be inferred in some way or other.

The task is enormous, and so was the outcome. The value of ecosystem services worldwide was assessed at almost twice the value of global production. What is this supposed to mean? That ecosystem services are immensely valuable, which no one would presumably doubt, but what guidance does it give to decision makers? Keep in mind that the value of global production is the sum of all incomes generated in the world. Ignoring credit creation, which cannot expand indefinitely, we can never pay for more than corresponds to the sum of all incomes. Are we supposed to lie down on our bellies and use all our income to pay for ecosystem services? Who will collect the payments? What would be left for such trivialities as food and shelter?

Exactly this point was raised in a comment by Kerry Smith.[11] He found the result less than helpful for decision makers and pointed out that it was supposed to be based on willingness to pay, which could not exceed the ability to pay in any meaningful way. The response by Constanza and co-authors was that if the value of the ecosystem were taken into account the world would have an entirely different price system and a different measure of gross domestic product.[12] Maybe so, but it is not easy to see how such a system could be implemented. Moreover, decision makers are living in the world as it is, not the world as it should be.

But this discussion points to a further problem with valuation of environmental goods that have no market value, such as recreational areas, wildlife as an object of adoration, and many other things. This valuation is based on the willingness to pay for these things. The willingness to pay must be estimated in some way; one and much-used method of doing so is to ask a representative sample of individuals how much they in fact are willing to pay. As a rule they do not have to pay anything in reality, which gives rise to two problems: (i) biased answers and (ii) overestimation. The reason for bias is obvious; anyone who knows that his answers could have a bearing on whether a certain wilderness area or animal species is to be protected is likely to tailor his answers to suit the outcome he desires; after all there is nothing to lose and something to gain. The reason for overestimation is that the same dollar can be used over and over again to pay for preserving things that some people feel should be preserved. This is serious because on the other side of the ledger are real and not just imaginary effects; food or other products derived from animals (whales or seals, for example) to be protected from exploitation and livelihoods that go with it or farming in areas to be set aside as wilderness.

This is well illustrated by the French wolf story above. The value of the wolves resides in the imagination of city dwellers who are enamored by wolves as wild animals at a suitable distance, but whatever value they might put on them we can be sure they will never have to pay; at any rate there is no such mechanism in place currently, nor has it been proposed. The losses are borne by the sheep rangers and the taxpayers who compensate the rangers for some of their monetary loss. The losses are real while the gains are imaginary, which is why the so-called willingness to pay methods to value wildlife and much else would be more appropriately labeled fantasy valuation rather than non-market valuation. Using these methods extensively we might end up with the logical absurdity of abstaining from using all those things that give rise to our entire production and still have some money left to preserve yet more "environmental amenities."[13]

THE CHARISMATIC MEGAFAUNA

Much of the concern about biodiversity probably stems from adoration of large animals such as lions, tigers, and other top predators. The World Wildlife Fund came into being after a series of newspaper articles in 1960 by Sir Julian Huxley, the first director of UNESCO, about how the wildlife of Eastern Africa was threatened with extinction.[14] A subsequent advertisement in the tabloid *Daily Mirror* raised a substantial sum of money.

For obvious reasons this attitude is mainly found among people who seldom encounter these animals except under controlled and protected circumstances, such as the Norwegian city dwellers who adore the bears and the wolves. The tourist industry in Africa organizes "safaris" where tourists view lions and other wildlife from the protected platforms of jeeps and go to the loo at night with armed guards at their side. In earlier times, the megafauna (large animals such as tigers and lions, but also grazing animals like the elephant and even large birds) was either a welcome and easily spotted source of food, or an unwelcome competitor and sometimes an outright danger and treated as such. As humans settled islands and whole continents much of the megafauna became extinct. After the ecosystem got perturbed by the invasion of humans it sought a new equilibrium; the humans preyed on the megafauna and some species could no longer survive. The American indigenous horse and mammoth disappeared, and so did several large birds and marsupials in Australia and New Zealand. Some ecologists now argue for "rewilding" these places by reintroducing the megafauna through animals such as the elephant which would, in that particular case, replace the mammoth.[15] Why so? Americans, Canadians, and Australians seem to have been doing just fine without them. In order to revive some "pristine" ecological state? We should probably be grateful that reviving the dinosaurs is not possible.

Whales and seals deserve a special mention in the context of "iconic" animals worthy of preservation as such rather than resources to be exploited. The campaign against whaling and seal hunting was high on the agenda of many environmental organizations in the 1970s and 1980s, Greenpeace in particular, and a solid fund-raiser. It is still ongoing, but with less intensity; the whaling industry is virtually dead. So is seal hunting; the ban on imports of seal skins into the United States and the European Union has seen to that. The major losers have been the huntsmen of Greenland and Canada who had few alternative means of livelihood. Nowadays the rest of us can easily do without the products of whaling and seal hunting, but it bears noting that seals eat fish, as do some whales, and that whales eat plankton which is also eaten by fish. Humanity derives a non-trivial part of its food supplies from fish, for which the seals and the whales compete with us, many of the latter indirectly. If the proponents of "ecosystem-based management" of fisheries and "ecosystem services" were serious and not just promoting an environmentalist agenda they would support the idea that, perhaps, whales and seals should be culled to support our fisheries, but the reader will be hard pressed to find traces of that.

WHALES

Nothing illustrates better the transition from the struggle for life to pampered environmentalism than the fate of whaling. Whales were a source of food and materials; the meat could be eaten and the fat cooked to provide oil, which was used for lighting, lubricating, and even as ingredients in soap and perfumes. The bones also had various uses. Whale hunting required daring and skills and lots of capital and was correspondingly rewarding. Whalers sailed from New England in the 1800s around Cape Horn to Alaska and back and made fortunes. In the 1600s the Dutch set up whaling stations in Spitsbergen, islands in the far and inhospitable north. As late as the 1960s large fleets from Europe hunted whales in the Southern Ocean. The Icelandic word for a windfall gain is "hvalreki:" beaching of whales. Two hundred years ago the Icelanders were mired in poverty and had only small, open rowboats, entirely unsuited to hunt whales. But whales that had drifted ashore could be butchered and used for food. That this could be a major bonanza says something about the living conditions at the time. Even a down to earth Icelandic poet of the twentieth century used the metaphor "no one knows who will eat a whale yet unborn."

From the modern viewpoint of sustainability, getting our oil and materials from living creatures like whales would seem ideal. They could be a lasting source of these things, provided enough of them were left to breed to produce new generations of whales. But the number of whales that the world oceans can support is limited, and so is the sustainable production of meat and oil which the whales could support. It surely is several orders of magnitude less than our demand for these things. So a vigorous whaling industry would not go very far in achieving an overall goal of sustainable development.

Today the whaling industry is anything but vigorous, but its troubles started long before the modern environmental campaigns against it. Sustainable whaling, like sustainable fishing, requires limiting the captures of whales to what the whale populations can support. The individual whaler has no incentives to do so, any more than the individual fisherman has an incentive to spare any fish; in a competition among many without individual property rights to fish or whales any whale or fish left behind simply means that it will be available for someone else to capture. Whale populations in various parts of the world were successively hunted to near- or full extinction. Thus the whaling industry was a bit like mining; when one population had been depleted the industry moved on to another.

When oil was discovered in Pennsylvania it first replaced whale oil in lamps. It has been argued that this discovery came in the nick of time, as whale oil was getting scarce because of overexploitation of the whale stocks.

Then the whaling industry moved to the Southern Ocean, but by the 1960s the populations of large whales had been depleted. In the meantime an international body to manage whale stocks (the International Whaling Commission) had been established, but was rather ineffectual in dealing with the overexploitation problem. Finally, around 1970, when the industry was disappearing because of lack of profitability, the International Whaling Commission agreed on a moratorium on the most depleted stocks in the Southern Ocean.

But other things were afoot. Scientists had studied whales and discovered an elaborate signaling system of sounds they presumably used for navigation and communication among themselves. High intelligence was ascribed to these animals. Whale songs were recorded and played. An interest in whales as living creatures developed. Fictions and myths about them multiplied; films were made and books written for children and adults. Over time, whales came to be regarded as special and in effect as holy animals by many and perhaps even most people in the western world. Killing whales for profit was considered as something of a crime. Their status became similar to that of cows in Hinduism and rooted in a similar superstition. We have now reached the point where the United States threatens nations who engage in whaling with trade sanctions. Public officials from New Zealand got in trouble a few years ago when they were reported having tasted whale delicacies at a conference dinner in Japan. It probably helps that mankind does not critically depend on whaling or whale products; opposition to both demands few sacrifices from anyone. What would happen if India gets rich and Hindus begin to proselytize the sacredness of cows could turn out to be interesting to watch.

The position of whales in modern western society is well illustrated, in all its weirdness, by the story of Keiko. This was a killer whale, captured at a young age (probably three years) off Iceland and put into a local aquarium. After a few years he was sold to Canada and then on to Mexico City. He did his tricks so well that he starred in several movies under the name of Willy; the first hit was *Free Willy*, and then there were more. But that was a committing title—the story was about a boy releasing a captive killer whale—so on the initiative from the moviemaker (Warner Bros.) a foundation was established to support him with the ultimate purpose of bringing him back to the wild. The foundation attracted sufficient money to keep a "Free Willy" circus going for years.

On his way back to the wild, Keiko was taken to the aquarium in Newport, Oregon, and in September 1998 flown by the United States Air Force to the Icelandic fishing village of Vestmannaeyjar in a bulky transportation plane. The local airport is small and notorious for winds, and the airplane had a difficult landing with a severe and costly damage to the landing gear. Keiko was unharmed, however, and put in a cage in the harbor. A crowd of experts and trainers accompanied him and set in train a program of integrating him into the wild. He was released from the cage and taken on excursions into the surroundings, but to begin with he always returned to the cage. Cynics took this as a sign of his intelligence; who would give up being fed for having to hunt for one's own food?

But maybe Keiko was not as smart as he was imagined to be; he disappeared, the trainers lost track of him, but he surfaced after two months off the coast of Norway. This was a bit ironic, Norway being one of few countries which defy opinion against whaling and allows whale hunting in its own waters. The excursion across the Atlantic had taken its toll on Keiko, whose hunting skills had never been much developed, so his handlers began feeding him again. In December 2002 Keiko died, not because he was hunted down by Norwegians (killer whales are not hunted in Norway), but apparently because of a lung disease. His cadaver was duly buried. Nearby there is a road sign pointing to his grave, for devotees that might want to pay him their respects.

NOTES

1. See Miller (1997), p. 14.
2. K. N. Ninnan (2009), p. 5.
3. See Brink (ed., 2011).
4. See Fitzsimmons (1999), chapter 6.
5. Reported in the *New York Times*, September 3, 2013.
6. See Fitzsimmons (1999), chapter 4.
7. See Lomborg (2001), chapter 23.
8. Lomborg (2001), p. 250.
9. Quoted in Kaufman (1994), pp. 175–76.
10. Published in *Nature*, Vol. 387, 1997, pp. 253–69, reprinted in Ladle (ed., 2009), Vol. I, pp. 690–708.
11. Published in *Regulation*, Vol. 20, No. 3, Summer 1997, pp. 16–17.
12. Their retort was published in *Regulation*, Vol. 20, No. 4, Fall 1997, pp. 2–3.
13. In technical terms, this is the issue behind using "compensated demand" rather than the market demand in calculating "consumer surplus." "Compensated demand" means that people are in principle supposed to actually pay for the benefits they derive from public goods, leaving them with less income than if they did not. Using market demand rather than compensated demand is likely to overstate people's willingness to pay for public goods.
14. See Haq and Paul (2012).
15. See Donlan, C. J. et al., "Pleistocene rewilding: an optimistic agenda for twenty-first century conservation," in Ladle (ed., 2009), Vol. I, pp. 447–85.

Chapter Five

Energy

The probability of finding oil underneath the North Sea is insignificant.

—Attributed to a prominent Norwegian geologist, around 1960

We cannot long continue our present rate of progress . . . it is useless to think of substituting any other fuel for coal.

—Stanley Jevons, *The Coal Question* (1865)

Secure provision of energy is arguably the most important issue for any developed society. The provision of abundant and cheap energy is the very basis of our way of life. It is cheap and abundant energy that makes it possible for us to grow and distribute our food, provides us with implements of various kinds which we could never make with our bare hands, allows us to heat or cool our houses and to travel around the globe. It is doubtful indeed if even hard core environmentalists would go without these amenities; in any case we see too few of them trying to survive in the bush on their own and out of touch with the rest of civilization. Yet the energy providers are prime targets of environmentalist agitation and propaganda.

Ever since the industrial revolution, our supply of energy has come predominantly from so-called fossil fuels; first coal, then oil and natural gas. This is still so; almost 90 percent of all our commercial primary energy comes from these sources, and this share has been relatively stable for a long time.[1] In the 1970s and 1980s nuclear power made great inroads, and the last 20 years or so wind power has done so too, although on a much smaller scale. Figure 5.1 illustrates this. We see that in the 1960s the share of fossil fuels was about 95 percent, but had fallen below 90 percent by 1990 and has remained fairly steady since then. The share of "other renewables" (that is, other than hydro-

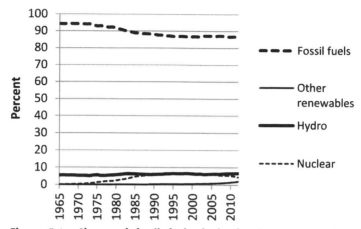

Figure 5.1. Shares of fossil fuels, hydroelectric power, nuclear power, and other (than hydro) renewables in production of primary energy. Source: *BP Statistical Review of World Energy.*

electric power) is less than 2 percent, and its rise in recent years has mainly been at the expense of nuclear energy. Much of this is in fact geothermal energy, so that wind and solar energy are even less significant than the curve for "other renewables" suggests. They have, however, grown rapidly in recent years, but whether that will be maintained remains to be seen.

In chapter 3 there is a diagram (Figure 3.2) of the production of oil since the Second World War. It is on a logarithmic scale, so that the steadily rising first part of the curve shows an even growth rate, which amounted to no less than 12 percent per year. A part of this was due to the inroads oil was making on coal, the traditional fuel of the industrial revolution. The figure also shows the price of oil, in a constant value of money. The low and falling price of oil until the early 1970s is conspicuous, apart from the first years after the Second World War. Most of this period was one of unprecedented economic growth and improving living standards in the industrialized part of the world, and it went hand in hand with an unprecedented increase in the consumption of oil. It came to an abrupt halt in the 1970s with the Arab oil embargo (1973) and the revolution in Iran (1978–1979). Both interrupted the flow of oil only slightly, but the world had become so oil-dependent that the price of oil went through the roof. The growth in consumption of oil did not resume its former strength even if the price fell drastically in 1986 and remained low until early this century.

The predominance of fossil fuels in the energy supplies of the world is an inconvenient fact for those who believe that emissions of carbon dioxide cause global warming on a scale that will have dire consequences. These emissions are primarily due to the use of fossil fuels. Figure 5.2 shows the

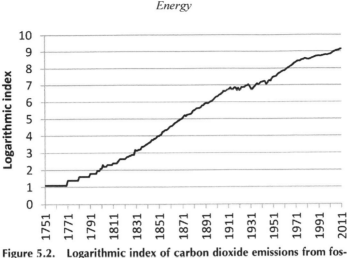

Figure 5.2. Logarithmic index of carbon dioxide emissions from fossil fuels and cement production. Source: U.S. Department of Energy, Carbon Dioxide Information Analysis Center.

emissions of carbon dioxide from fossil fuels and cement production since 1751. It is on a logarithmic scale, so the evenly rising portions of the curve imply an even rate of growth. There are three periods of even and rapid growth, late 1770s to the First World War, end of the Second World War to the mid-1970s, and the years of this century. All three are periods of steady and rapid economic growth and improving living standards, the first due to the spread of the industrial revolution, the second the golden years in the western world after the Second World War, and the third the spectacular rise of China. Note also the jagged period flanked by the two world wars. This covers the world depression (the 1930s) and the two world wars. So now we know what to do in case we want to get serious about the emissions of greenhouse gases. Fortunately, the world leaders seem to be preoccupied with something entirely different.

The global warming issue has now been on the agenda for about two decades; at the environmental summit meeting in Rio 1992 many countries pledged to reduce their emissions of greenhouse gases. Yet very little has happened since other than greenhouse gas emissions have continued and even increased. Fossil fuels are still by far the dominant source of energy, as we have seen. There is, of course, a very good reason why this is so; fossil fuels are still by far the cheapest and most convenient source of energy in almost all uses. Gasoline and diesel oil pack more energy into a given tank volume than any other fuel and are in addition very easy to handle, they can be pumped or poured and do not evaporate at atmospheric pressure like natural gas would. In contrast with hydrogen, they pollute the atmosphere, but hydrogen is not a primary source of energy and must be produced from other sources. Only if hydrogen is produced from, say, hydroelectric power does it have a clear environmental advantage over diesel and gasoline, but it is much more difficult to handle and to store.

Nevertheless, the media and the propaganda machines of various environmental organizations busy themselves with discussions about renewable energy as the thing that will save the world. This is not just a harmless illusion but also a wasteful one, since the money spent on these "solutions" could be put to a better use. So what is wrong with renewable energy? It can be summarized in two words, intermittency and dispersion.

Intermittency means that the energy is not available when we need it. The wind does not always blow, and sometimes it is even too strong for the wind turbines to cope with. To make matters worse, in some parts of the world, Europe in particular, calm weather often coincides with severe cold when people need energy to heat their homes. Solar power is also intermittent; the sun does not shine at night, and in some parts of the world it is not necessarily seen during the day either. There is yet no technology available for storing large amounts of energy, so solar and wind power make it necessary to invest in power plants which can back them up. Such power sources are—you may have guessed it—fossil fuels, primarily natural gas. This need for backup capacity necessarily makes wind and solar power more expensive and is one of the reasons why they cannot compete with coal or natural gas in the production of electricity. What makes them economically viable nonetheless are government subsidies or requirements that power companies buy a certain amount of "sustainable" energy. In any case these costs are borne by the general public, either in the form of taxes or of a higher price of electricity.

Dispersion comes from the lack of energy density per unit area and the consequent demand on space, sometimes to the detriment of food production or other uses of the same space, including aesthetic ones. The United Kingdom is one of the countries that have opted for wind power as a substantial part of the solution for its energy requirements. How much space would the UK need to satisfy its electricity needs? In 2011 the production of electricity in the UK was 368 TWh (terawatt hours). The population of the UK was 63.2 million in 2011, so this comes to 16 kWh (kilowatt hours) per day per person $[(368*10^{12})/(365*63.2*10^{6}) = 16*10^{3}$ Wh]. In an informative and delightfully readable book, *Renewable Energy without the Hot Air*, physics professor David MacKay provides interesting numbers. If 10 percent of Britain were set aside for wind turbines this could produce 20 kWh per day per person.[2] Alternatively, a strip four kilometers wide all around Britain and filled with turbines would deliver 16 kWh per day per person.[3] So, it is not inconceivable that the UK could produce electricity equal to its current use from wind, but at a high cost, over lots of space, and with a need for large backup capacity.

But the story of transition to renewable energy is longer than that. Currently Britons heat their houses with gas and travel by car. To replace this with electricity it would have to increase from the current 16 kWh per day per person to more than 100 kWh per day per person.[4] That is a long haul. Could solar come to the rescue? Here is MacKay again: If 5 percent of Britain's territory were set aside for photovoltaic solar panels, it could produce 50 kWh per day per person.[5] He proposes solar panels in the Sahara as a better and probably a necessary complementary option. Cheap it would not be, and what about the security problems? Would the current have been cut during the Libyan revolution of 2011? During the disturbances in Algeria in the 1990s? What about Northern Mali? The countries with sovereignty over the Sahara are not known for their political stability.

The most difficult transition from fossil fuels will undoubtedly be the substitution for jet fuel. A battery driven airplane may be a technical possibility, but would probably be full of batteries and empty of passengers. Again, because of its energy density and easy handling, liquid fuels probably are the only option for air travel. Liquid fuels can be derived from plants, but here again we run into the problem of dispersion. Replacing ten percent of the American consumption of oil with ethanol from corn would require 10 percent of all currently used farmland in the United States, so replacing it all with corn-based ethanol would leave nothing at all for food production (assuming, for the sake of the argument, that corn can be grown anywhere, which is not possible).[6] Admittedly, corn probably is the worst option, but even switchgrass is not much better; sugar ethanol is probably the most effective liquid plant-based fuel. Even if we only were to replace jet fuel with plant-based liquids, the risk is that this would be at the expense of food production, or by turning the rain forests of the Amazon and elsewhere into sugar plantations.

Not only would biofuels cut into food production; many scientists have argued that the greenhouse gas advantage of biofuels is doubtful and possibly nonexistent. Mark Delucchi, research scientist at the University of California Davis, who specializes in greenhouse gas emissions, puts it this way: "To avoid these problems [associated with production of biofuels], biofuel feedstocks will have to be grown on land that has no alternative commercial use and no potential alternative ecological benefits, in areas with ample rainfall or groundwater, and with little or no inputs of fertilizers, chemicals and fossil fuels. . . . It is not clear that it can be done economically and sustainably at large scales."[7] The last is surely an understatement if ever there was one.

In these lofty ideas about getting our energy from the land we should recognize our past; this is in fact what we used to do. Mankind used horses and other draft animals to travel, to till the soil, to cut the grass, and to harvest its crops. For this purpose land had to be set aside for growing the necessary fodder to feed these animals. If we still did this we would need a lot more land than we now use to feed the seven billion of us. In 1915 the American horse population reached its maximum, with one-third of all agricultural land used to feed them.[8] Those who put value on undisturbed nature as habitat for wild animals or whatever ought to ponder this; without fossil fuels there would be much less undisturbed nature left. Perhaps fossil fuels are not the environmentalist's worst enemy after all.

And here is yet another argument in favor of fossil fuels. People in poor countries use dung and wood as fuel for cooking and burn it in open fires indoors. In fact, people in what now are rich countries did this not so many generations ago. Open indoor fires emit smoke that is meant to escape through a hole in the roof, but much of it lingers inside and those who spend much time in the smoke-filled kitchen, typically women and children, contract respiratory diseases. Such diseases have been listed as the second most important cause of premature deaths in the world, next after HIV/AIDS and ahead of tuberculosis and malaria.[9] In many countries, transition from dung and firewood to kerosene would be among the most welfare-enhancing developments one could think of. And then there are the trees that would be saved by not using fuelwood.

IS OUR ENERGY USE SUSTAINABLE?

Professor MacKay dedicated his book "to those who will not have the benefits of two billion years' accumulated energy reserves." This is the energy dilemma in a nutshell. The bane of renewable energy is dispersion. But fossil fuels were originally produced by photosynthesis which was just as dispersed as it always has been; what has made them so dense is the immense time and geological force turning the debris into hydrocarbons with highly concentrated energy content. So, burning fossil fuels means living off inherited capital.

Is living off inherited capital sustainable? It depends on how much was inherited, the use rate, and the life span of the heir. It is not difficult to imagine one or a few generations of heirs living comfortably off the estate. Human civilization is not going to last forever. How long will the fossil fuels last? We simply do not know. For decades we have found more oil and gas than we burn. For decades we have had enough proven oil reserves for more than 40 years at the current use rate. Of natural gas we have enough for 60 years, and of coal for several hundred. Fossil fuels are in principle a given inventory but in practice more like goods in the supermarket; when the shelves are empty the delivery trucks come with more. Neither governments nor private companies have an unlimited amount of money to spend on prospecting for oil or gas; when the reserves go down they go out and find more. So far they have been quite successful, and even if reserves get depleted in one place, new provinces open up, sometimes unexpectedly. And then there is technology. Technological progress has increased the recoverable reserves of oil and gas enormously by making it possible to recover a larger share of oil and gas in each location and by making new locations accessible. Oil is now being extracted off the shore of Brazil through five kilometers deep wells, below two kilometers of ocean. The latest revolutionary change is the new drilling technology that has made shale oil and gas accessible and increased the reserves of the United States to the extent that the Americans talk about self-sufficiency in the near future.

That said, the risk is that human civilization will outlast the burning of all fossil fuels. Then, if living standards are to be maintained, other sources of energy will have to be developed. Renewable sources such as wind and solar have their serious limitations, as already discussed, and are unlikely to be sufficient to maintain the living standards we have grown accustomed to, let alone any further improvement that might occur while we still can draw on the fossil fuels. What, then, could come to the rescue? It is difficult to see how we can avoid relying mostly on nuclear energy. Nuclear reactors can produce electricity reasonably cheaply and reliably from a limited amount of fissile material (uranium and thorium). Nuclear power plants do not demand much space; replacing a nuclear power plant with wind power would require an area that is 500 times larger.[10] Even if uranium and thorium are finite and not renewable resources, they would probably suffice to supply the world with energy for hundreds and possibly thousands of years.

Given the hype about global warming, it is indeed surprising to see the opposition to nuclear power, probably the only credible alternative to fossil energy. Paradoxically, the most outspoken opponents of nuclear power often are the same people who are most concerned about global warming. Just as renewable energy, nuclear energy does not produce any carbon dioxide emissions, and it does not need a backup because of intermittency. Some environmentalists concerned about global warming have indeed drawn the inescapable conclusion and come out in support of nuclear energy.

Not surprisingly, the opposition to nuclear energy is based on distortion of facts verging on superstition. There are two major arguments against nuclear energy, the risk of accidents and the storage of residual material that stays dangerously radioactive for a long time. To begin with the latter, spent uranium fuel contains dangerously radioactive material which has to be stored for thousands of years at safe enough sites to prevent it from leaking into the surroundings. This can only be done in areas safe from earthquakes and other disruptive geological events. Such areas have been identified and in a few cases taken into use, but the opposition has been fierce and, you guessed it, the precautionary principle frequently invoked. An additional problem is that plutonium, a component of the dangerous waste, is used in making nuclear bombs, with the attendant risk of spent fuel getting into the hands of terrorists or rogue governments.

As an alternative to storage, spent nuclear fuel can be reprocessed and turned into useable fissile material. This is already done in some countries. It is possible that a more sophisticated technology for reprocessing spent nuclear fuel could reduce the residue of long-time radioactive material so that the problem of storing it could be much reduced or eliminated. Another possible solution is thorium, which can be used in nuclear reactors instead of uranium. Thorium produces much less waste of long-lived radioactive material and is less useful as a source of weapons-grade fissile materials. It is much more abundant than uranium, but more expensive to use.

Then there is the risk of accidents. The problem with nuclear accidents is that they tend to be dramatic when they occur, but they do not occur very often. The two most famous ones are Chernobyl in what was then the Soviet Union and Fukushima in Japan. While the first was due to human error and perhaps less than an ideal design of the reactor itself, the Fukushima accident was brought about by a monstrous earthquake and the accompanying tsunami. This was an extremely rare event, and what appeared to be a carefully designed mechanism meant to be able to cope with earthquakes and tsunamis could not cope with this one. The damage caused by the release of radioactivity was considerable, but much less than what occurred after Chernobyl. The number of people killed by the Chernobyl disaster is controversial, because many deaths are caused by cancers erupting many years after the fact and which could have other causes, but in a long time perspective these deaths and even other damages are less than those associated with mining of coal and extraction of oil and gas. Every year thousands of people die in accidents in these industries, especially coal mining, but no one pays much attention because of the ongoing and small-scale character of these events. In many countries that rely heavily on nuclear power, such as Sweden and France, no fatal accidents have ever occurred in the nuclear power industry.

There are statistics to back this up. An EU-sponsored investigation related accidents to the amount of energy produced (GWy, gigawatt years).[11] The accident rate for nuclear power is less than 0.2. For coal it is above 2 and for oil it is above 4. Even wind exceeds nuclear, but only slightly.

Nevertheless, the mind-set brought about by the dramatic nuclear accidents and the wishful thinking that we can get our energy risk-free has thwarted further development of the nuclear power industry and even enticed some politicians to shut down what they already have. For many years Sweden had a plan to do this, despite decades of accident-free nuclear power production, but seems now to have found out that this would prove too costly. Germany decided on a plan to close down its nuclear power stations after the Fukushima accident, even if Germany is not earthquake prone and could not possibly be hit by a tsunami.

A discussion of what to do about the dilemma energy use versus global warming would not be complete without mentioning carbon capture and storage. This means taking the carbon dioxide out of oil, coal, or natural gas and storing it underground so that it does not leak into the atmosphere. Carbon capture and storage on a large scale is an unproven technology. It is used on some oil platforms where the captured carbon dioxide is pumped back into the oil fields to enhance the production of oil. There are three problems with carbon capture and storage applied to large power plants (usually coal fired). First, it is expensive and uses up a large part of the energy produced, maybe as much as 40 percent.[12] Second, the gas (carbon dioxide) must be stored securely underground so that it does not leak into the atmosphere. Third, transporting the captured carbon dioxide to locations identified as secure would be expensive; it would probably require pipelines such as those used for natural gas, but where nothing useful comes out at the end of the pipe. There has been fierce public resistance to the storage of carbon dioxide underground at proposed sites in the Netherlands and in Germany because of fear that it might leak out suddenly and accidentally. If it did, it could suffocate anyone happening to be in its way. A sudden and unexpected leakage of carbon dioxide from a volcanic lake in Cameroon in 1986 killed more than a thousand people. This has been taken as an example of what could happen if carbon dioxide would leak from its underground storage.

But perhaps the future will bring solutions that we can only dream of today. In August 2013 David Hendricks, of *San Antonio Express-News*, reported on a plant, under construction, designed to produce marketable products from carbon dioxide, such as baking soda and hydrochloric acid (used in fracking). Will it be a flop or a harbinger of things to come? We do not yet know. And George Olah, Nobel Laureate in chemistry, believes that captured carbon could be transformed into methanol and used as motor fuel cheaply enough to be commercially viable.[13]

What could prolong the age of fossil fuels by hundreds and possibly thousands of years is the frozen methane on and underneath the sea bottom. This is known under various names, methane clathrates and methane hydrates being two of them. No one has yet found out how these deposits could be turned into commercial energy, but research is ongoing in various countries. Meanwhile, we must do with what we have. What is exceedingly ill taken is to let vicarious environmental arguments get in the way of extracting fossil fuels easily accessible with known and proven technology. A case in point is the American Arctic National Wildlife Refuge (ANWR). This is located on the so-called North Slope of Alaska, bordering on the Arctic Ocean. It is a desolate, flat piece of land, useless for anything other than digging up the riches underneath. A meter or so of the topsoil thaws during the short, Arctic summer, sustaining some grass which in turn sustains caribou herds. Underneath are hundreds of meters of permafrost. The term "wildlife refuge" must be a feat of salesmanship, calculated to give the impression that this poor wildlife (mainly caribou) has nowhere else to go. Adjacent to ANWR are the oil fields on the North Slope, the two largest ones in North America. The oil installations are scattered over a gigantic area and connected by pipelines above ground; the caribou roam freely around and sometimes shelter underneath the pipelines, as anyone taking the trouble to travel to this area can see for himself. In the winter the oil workers must take care not to be attacked by polar bears that come onshore; the ocean is covered with ice in winter. Those who do not have time or money to travel to the North Slope can consult a publication documenting the coexistence of oil extraction and wildlife in the oil fields of the North Slope; unexpectedly, perhaps, the wildlife seems to thrive better with the oil fields than it did without them.[14] Unfortunately and undeservedly, ANWR apparently has become a fetish among many people who probably have only dim ideas of what they are talking about. Worse, a representative of the Wilderness Society is on record for saying the ANWR is needed "just to have it there."[15] Advancing rational arguments in that context has the same effect as throwing water on the proverbial goose.

NOTES

1. According to the *BP Statistical Review of World Energy*. This publication considers only commercial energy. The IEA (International Energy Agency) also includes noncommercial energy such as subsistence biomass in poor countries. This raises the share of renewable energy in the IEA statistics, but fuelwood and dung is not what the proponents of renewable energy in affluent countries are talking about. Otherwise there are few discrepancies between the two sources, except how they convert hydroelectric power into oil equivalents; in the BP statistics hydroelectric power is about as important as nuclear power, but in the IEA statistics it is much less. What is called "energy" in these sources as well as in this book does not comprise the energy we get from the food we eat or the draught animals we might use, only the energy that we produce in various ways and for such various purposes as heating or cooling, transportation, production of goods, and so on.

2. MacKay (2009), p. 33.

3. MacKay (2009), p. 61.

4. See MacKay (2009), chapter 27.

5. MacKay (2009), p. 41.

6. See Bryce (2010).

7. Quoted from Idso, Carter, and Singer (eds., 2011), p. 400. The carbon neutrality of biofuels is discussed at some length in Morriss et al. (2011), p. 62 ff. and p. 218.

8. Ridley (2010), p. 140.

9. See *World Energy Outlook 2010*, International Energy Agency, Paris, Figure 8.5.

10. Based on MacKay (2009), p. 167.

11. Quoted from MacKay (2009), p. 168. Bolch and Lyons (1993, pp. 110–11) also report interesting comparative numbers on safety of nuclear power.

12. Quoted in Sondergaard (2009), p. 199. See also pp. 303–5.

13. See op-ed piece in the *Wall Street Journal*, October 11, 2013.

14. See Truett and Johnson (eds., 2000), especially pp. 401–8.

15. Quoted in George Reisman, *The Toxicity of Environmentalism*, in *Man and Nature*, The Foundation for Economic Education, Irvington-on-Hudson, New York, 1993, p. 94.

Chapter Six

Global Warming, Forest Death, and the Ozone Hole

Question from an unidentified woman: "Vice President Al Gore, what issues caused by climate change globally are likely to affect the United States security *in the next ten years?*" (emphasis added).

Gore: "You know, even a one meter increase, even a three foot increase in the sea level would cause tens of millions of climate refugees. If Greenland were to break up and slip into the sea or West Antarctica, or half of either or half of both, it would be a 20-feet increase, and that would lead to more than 450 million climate refugees."

> —Al Gore on *Larry King Live*, May 22, 2007, later honored with the Nobel Peace Prize for his informative work on global warming. Quoted from Michaels and Balling, Jr. (2009), p. 1

The evidence in support of these predictions [of global cooling] has now begun to accumulate so massively that meteorologists are hard-pressed to keep up with it . . . resulting famines could be catastrophic. . . the most devastating outbreak of tornadoes ever recorded. . . droughts, floods, extended dry spells, long freezes, delayed monsoons. . . impossible for starving peoples to migrate. . . the present decline has taken the planet about a sixth of the way toward the Ice Age.

> —Newsweek, April 28, 1975

In the previous chapter I discussed energy dilemmas. These dilemmas occur because we are critically dependent on fossil fuels, but burning these fuels releases carbon dioxide, which is alleged to cause global warming. In this chapter I discuss the global warming issue. I then move on to forest death, an issue of much concern in the 1980s, but one that has gone away, partly because it was overblown and overhyped by the media and partly because the underlying problem, release of sulfur dioxide, has largely been resolved. There are parallels with the carbon dioxide problem; the media hype is one, the possible removal of the unwelcome gas another, but for carbon dioxide the removal is much more costly and probably not economically feasible. Lastly I discuss the ozone hole problem, which has certain obvious parallels with the global warming problem, except that it is immensely more easy to deal with.

GLOBAL WARMING

Is the world getting warmer? In the words of one scientist who claims, and convincingly so, to try to be unbiased, "[t]he straightforward answer is that this depends entirely on the means of measurement and time span that is being examined and compared."[1] It is well known that the global temperature has been rising since the end of the Little Ice Age. I grew up close to Europe's largest glacier. With a not so slight exaggeration, I could say I saw it shrink before my eyes. But I later came to know that this glacier had been smaller, and perhaps much smaller, several hundred years ago.

The Doomsday prophets of the global warming crowd have avoided the main pitfall of *The Limits to Growth*; the climate predictions are for the long term and will not come true or untrue until after those who now are making them are dead, while the authors of *The Limits to Growth* turned out to have been mistaken within their lifetime. One thing the global warming studies and *The Limits to Growth* have in common is that both are based on model simulations. The scientific basis of the climate models is, however, of an entirely different magnitude. While *The Limits to Growth* was without any scientific foundation whatsoever except for prolongation of exponential trends, the Intergovernmental Panel on Climate Change (IPCC) uses a number of elaborate climate simulation models based on meteorological science. Behind each of these models is a large group of scientists whose work has been thoroughly peer reviewed.

The problem with the climate models and their predictions is not that they are "wrong" or represent a deliberate conspiracy among scientists seeking to milk research funds. There may be, and probably is, some of this going on, but the scientific criticism of these models, and the work of the IPCC in general, has been vigorous and is likely to have weeded out many if not all their faults. Admittedly, some of this criticism has been from the outside of the "climate community" and highly unwelcome. One example is the infamous hockey stick episode, another is a climate scientist saying when asked to provide data on temperature history: "We have 25 years or so invested in the work. Why should I make the data available to you, when your aim is to try and find something wrong with it?"[2]

The problem with the predictions of the climate models is that they are not well grounded in actual experience; they are based on heating effects of certain gases and magnifying feedback effects the strength of which are disputed. Despite all rhetoric to the contrary, this science is not at all settled, and it is not difficult to find reputable climate scientists who dispute the strength of the man-made warming effects and even their existence altogether.[3] Those who tout the language of a "settled science" are politicians and other proselytizers who have never been anywhere near a scientific carrier and whose knowledge of science is rudimentary at best. The "science is settled" turn of phrase is the language of the Inquisition. Climate scientists worth their salt have a more humble attitude. Here is what Philip Jones, director of the Climate Research Unit at the University of East Anglia and no climate skeptic, said when answering the question whether the debate on climate change is over:

> It would be a supposition on my behalf to know whether all scientists who say the debate is over are saying that for the same reason. I don't believe the vast majority of scientists think this. This is not my view. There is still much that needs to be undertaken to reduce uncertainties, not just for the future, but for the instrumental (and especially the paleoclimatic) past as well.[4]

As the climate scientists would be the first to admit, there is enormous uncertainty surrounding the predictions of all climate models. As an example, the worst global warming scenario in the IPCC report from 2007 predicts an increase in surface temperature of 4 degrees (Celsius) by the year 2100, but also shows a band of possible increases in that same scenario from about 2 to 6 degrees (the most recent one of 2013 has modified this downwards, but only slightly). The temperature increases in all scenarios, also those that stabilize the greenhouse gases in the atmosphere, have bands of possible increases that to some extent overlap.

The greatest uncertainty, however, pertains to the consequences of global warming and what we can and will do about them. Two degrees change in average global temperature does not sound like a great deal, but could in fact mean formidable changes in climate. In some places it does not take a large change in rainfall to make growing of certain crops impossible. Irrigation could, of course, be a solution, but less rainfall in places that now are sources of water for irrigation could in fact severely constrain existing irrigation facilities. Some areas where there is now productive farmland could become arid and unusable. On the other hand, new areas which now cannot be used could open up. Permafrost will thaw in some places, and the autumn frosts will come later in some places and make it possible to grow crops that now cannot be grown. What the balance would be we know little or nothing about. One problem is that we have little or no experience of a climate change of the magnitude that some of the climate scenarios predict. But we do have some. We have the so-called Little Ice Age of Europe which began in the 1300s and seems to have been particularly cold in the 1600s. That was not a happy time; crop harvests fell or failed in many places, with the associated famines. The Norse settlement in Greenland died out, probably because the harvests failed and the grass did not grow, and the Icelanders nearly perished as well. It appears that the climate in Scandinavia over a few hundred years before and after 1000 AD was as warm as or warmer than it is now. The harvests probably became more bountiful, enabling more people to survive. This in turn is likely to have created a surplus of angry young men with no land to farm. A surplus of angry young men with nothing to do but mischief spells trouble, and in pre-1000 Scandinavia the result was the Viking age.

In other parts of the world there have been changes in climate of a similar magnitude or greater. There are stories of states or civilizations which disappeared because a change in climate destroyed the agriculture which supported them. In other cases, states and civilizations rose and flourished because of an advantageous change in climate. We do well to notice that the climate has always been variable for reasons having nothing to do with human activity, and humanity has always had to adjust to changes in climate. The difference now is that we are infinitely better equipped than our ancestors to cope with such changes. The Doomsayers of global warming are fond of pointing out that those who will be hardest hit by climate change are the poorest countries in the world. True enough, and to escape from poverty and be better able to cope with problems of global warming, or any other problem for that matter, they will have to grow and develop industrially. That requires a huge increase in the use of energy, which primarily will have to come from fossil fuels. This, needless to say, will further increase the concentration of greenhouse gases in the atmosphere and so contribute to global warming.

Some environmentalists would appear to deny that rich countries will be better able to deal with the effects of global warming, or any disadvantageous climate change for that matter, than were our ancestors thousands of years ago. Brian Fagan, professor of anthropology, has this to say about the disappearance of Doggerland, now on the bottom of the North Sea: "Ten millennia ago, the inhabitants of Doggerland could adjust effortlessly to a changing world. Today, we are catastrophically vulnerable to attacks from the rising ocean and its tempests."[5] The naivety is incredible. How did the inhabitants of Doggerland adjust? They were stone age hunters and gatherers, roaming around in small bands where the inbreeding was probably ameliorated by fighting other bands, killing the menfolk and enslaving their women. Maybe they didn't notice the sea creeping up on them; that would have happened gradually, and if they noticed it would have been by finding their hunting grounds of yester-year inaccessible. So they would have had to hunt elsewhere, which probably would have increased their exposure to other unfriendly bands. Or maybe it just increased the opportunity to diversify their genes.

Is this just baseless speculation about the behavior of our primitive ancestors about whom we have no written record? Probably not; we do have written records of how this "tradition" may have lived on. In the Bible we read the following: Moses had sent his troops to take vengeance on the Midianites, at the behest of the Lord. Killing every man was not good enough. The returning soldiers brought back captives. "Moses was angry with the officers of the army . . .. Have you allowed all the women to live? They were the ones who followed Balaam's advice and enticed the Israelites to be unfaithful to the Lord . . .. Now kill all the boys. And kill every woman who has slept with a man, but save for yourselves every girl who has never slept with a man."[6] Records of similar events, many of an even more recent vintage, could probably fill a whole book. And there are some archaeological indications. At Talheim in Germany five thousand years ago a small community was wiped out, except that female skeletons are missing. Matt Ridley speculates they were abducted for much the same reason we can read about in the narratives from Moses.[7]

There are indications that people of times past had to deal with a climate change more rapid than the modern climate modelers like to talk about as "anthropogenic" and "unprecedented." The slide from the first warming after the last Ice Age into what is known as the Younger Dryas may have involved a cooling of seven degrees (Celsius) spread over a few decades or possibly even years, according to ice cores from the Greenland glacier. This seems to have nipped emerging agriculture in the Levant in the bud. The adjustment is unlikely to have been effortless, much less pleasant.[8]

The main reason why those of us who live in the rich countries of the world will be better able to deal with the challenges of global warming is that our economic activity and lifestyle is largely independent of the weather. Most of us work indoors on activities that are entirely independent of what the weather is like outside. Our main problem with the weather is getting to work and back if there is a snowstorm or ice on the roads. Global warming will not make that any worse and perhaps the opposite. It is, of course, true that we are ultimately dependent on the weather because of the crops we need to grow. While we might have to abandon some places we now farm, other places would open up, and the yields of the farms we now use could be affected and not only for the worse. The IPCC has considered the potential effect of global warming on farming and finds little change overall for a temperature rise up to two degrees (Celsius), but different areas could be affected in different ways. Increased carbon dioxide in the atmosphere is beneficial for plant growth and so has a positive effect, while other effects (drought, heat) are negative. With adaptation to climate change, yields of corn and wheat are expected to increase overall, while the yield of rice will stay constant. Little or no change is expected for pastures and livestock, except increased periodic heat stress. For warming beyond three degrees things begin to look less rosy.[9]

As a case in point, let us consider California. Any visitor to California surely envies its inhabitants for the benign climate and much else. Yet California is the last place on earth we would want to live if we were critically dependent on nature. Nothing grows without irrigation, and lacking the technology of modern civilization we would starve to death. When European settlers came to California the place was virtually empty of people and for a good reason. Modern California illustrates perfectly how modern technology has made us independent of weather and climate. Much of the food is imported, and the rest is grown with irrigation. Ironically, California seems to be a place with an inordinately high share of people who worry about global warming. Maybe they worry that for their part the climate can only change for the worse. While global warming will not make the rest of the world like California, the state is a good illustration of how technology can deal with possible consequences of climate change.

As discussed in the previous chapter, our modern technology is fueled with energy from oil, coal, and natural gas, all of which emit greenhouse gases in varying quantities. This has been so for several decades and is unlikely to change much for a long time to come. Insufficient recognition of this critical dependence on fossil fuels is perhaps the weakest point in the chain of reasoning by global warming alarmists. It is as simple as this: If we are to get serious about stopping global warming (to the extent it is happening and man-made) we would have to abandon most of our modern technology and go back to the lifestyle of the middle ages. How could that be? If greenhouse gases are warming the atmosphere, we have to stabilize the concentration of those gases. Stabilizing the concentration means limiting emissions to what the globe can absorb, which occurs through the photosynthesis of plants as well as absorption by the oceans. This capacity is about 20 percent of the emission level early this century, according to the *Stern Review*.[10] Other estimates state that the planet can absorb about a half of recent carbon dioxide emissions.[11] Ignoring for a moment both carbon capture and switch to energy sources with less or no emissions, this would mean a reduction in our energy use of 50–80 percent. Doing so would leave little room for driving or air travel, to say nothing of a further economic growth in rapidly developing countries like China. These countries are now in a phase where the use of energy grows faster than economic activity in general, while energy use grows less or not at all in the de-industrializing service-oriented economies of the rich countries, but due to the rapid growth of China and some other poor countries the emissions of carbon dioxide are rising fast.

It hardly needs to be said that an 80 percent decline in the use of fossil energy, and even 50 percent, is not going to happen overnight. If it happens, it will take a long time. There are several reasons for this. First, all countries except the very poorest have elaborate infrastructures which are geared to using a specific energy source; cars, airplanes, home heating equipment, and power plants, to name some. In some cases existing infrastructure can be modified—cars can be modified to run on natural gas or ethanol—but usually we would need to invest in entirely new equipment. Carbon capture and storage is an expensive and largely unproven technology which will take a long time to develop and may never succeed. Apart from its very high costs, a major problem is what to do with the captured carbon dioxide. Nuclear power has its own problems, but is otherwise the only serious alternative to fossil fuels. Hydroelectric and geothermal power stations can only be built where specific geographic and geological circumstances allow. Wind and solar power is still more expensive and totally insufficient as a single source. Anyone who thinks we can cut the use of fossil fuels to the extent we need to stabilize greenhouse gas concentration in the atmosphere unless we change our lifestyle beyond recognition is living in fantasyland.

Yet even serious publications sometimes report this fantasyland as being right around the bend. In its 2010 *World Energy Outlook*, the International Energy Agency held forth that the concentration of greenhouse gases in the atmosphere could be stabilized at 450 parts per million, a level some people think would suffice to limit the risk of global warming of two degrees (Celsius) to 50 percent. In about 20 years, or by 2035, the carbon dioxide emissions are supposed to be less than in 2009, after having risen moderately in the meantime. About two-thirds of the reduction, compared with a "business as usual" scenario, is supposed to come from less energy use and more energy efficiency. I invite my younger readers to return to this question in 2035.

Among the many follies of climate policy, those committed by Norway deserve mentioning. To begin with the basics, Norway is probably among those countries which would benefit and not lose from global warming. Summer temperatures are seldom uncomfortably high but winter is cold and miserable, so much so that Norway probably has the highest share of climate refugees in the world; that is, people who move to southern latitudes when they retire to escape the winter. Rising sea levels, a possible consequence of global warming, would be a small inconvenience for mountainous Norway. Norway's share of global greenhouse gas emissions is about two pro mille and thus insignificant. Yet Norwegian politicians have kept a high profile in fighting global warming. They have also spent a large sum of money for this purpose, sometimes with a doubtful outcome. Some of the oil and gas platforms in the North Sea use electric power from the mainland instead of natural gas, which is available on the spot (sometimes there even are idle gas turbines in place). This reduces Norway's own emissions of carbon dioxide but has a less impressive overall effect; the gas not burnt on the platforms will ultimately be burnt somewhere in Europe where it is exported. When there is a shortage of hydroelectric power in Norway, as happens now and then because of uneven rainfall, electricity is imported from coal-fired power stations in Denmark. Norway has donated a large sum of money to a fund for preserving rain forests. The rain forests are located in some of the most corrupt countries in the world, so making sure the money serves its purpose will be a challenge. And who cuts, or burns, the rain forests? People, often of small means, who are trying to make a better living for themselves and their families by growing crops or raising cattle for which there is high and increasing demand in a world of an increasing population and rising incomes. The rich and industrially developed countries of the world have long since cut down most of their forests to make place for their cities and farms. They are now paying those that aspire to follow in their footsteps to stay behind.

The uncertainties in climate policy have to do with the effects of global warming and whether and to what extent it is man-made. The only certainties are the costs of reducing greenhouse gas emissions. They are formidable, and getting serious about global warming to the extent the believers prescribe would change the lifestyle in rich countries beyond recognition and lock the poor countries of the world into continued poverty. It is, to say the least, highly unlikely to happen, nor is it desirable.

THE FOREST DEATH HYPE

Those who remember the 1980s will remember reports about acid rain and forest death. And they will also recall that, for some reason, this issue disappeared from the mainstream media in the 1990s. What happened?

Acid rain is caused by emissions of sulfur dioxide from burning coal and oil in power plants and motor vehicles. Sulfur dioxide is an obnoxious substance, although useful in miniscule quantities; among other things it is involved in wine making. As we sip our wine we would not think of it and neither do we notice, but sulfur dioxide is foul smelling and a health hazard in large quantities. Sulfur dioxide mixes with water vapor in clouds and falls to the ground as acid rain. It can acidify lakes to the extent that fish cannot survive and, so it was alleged, acidify the soil so that trees cannot survive.

The hypothesis that acid rain kills forests originated in Germany and enthralled the German public in particular in the 1970s and 1980s.[12] Two German weeklies, *Der Spiegel* and *Der Stern*, hyped in 1981 that all German forests would be dead in three to five years. The issue gave a major boost to the German Green party. In most other countries the issue caused less concern, but in Norway it was given a high profile. Acid rain in Norway is caused by sulfur emissions in other countries, the United Kingdom in particular, and the Norwegian government was involved in discussions about this issue with the UK government. The forest death theory was a convenient argument. Norwegian foresters who did not buy into the forest death theory were summoned to government ministers and encouraged to improve their research. Those who refused and put their scientific integrity above everything else were ostracized and experienced problems with their careers. And Norway was not the only place where such shenanigans happened. A comprehensive study of forest death in the United States and Canada found no evidence of forest death being caused by acid rain. This was unwelcome news for the US Environmental Protection Agency, which tried to suppress the finding.[13] Of more recent vintage, in the United States there are cases of climate scientists being inconvenienced or fired, at the behest of politicians, for expressing "climate-skeptic" views.[14]

The trees are still standing, however. So what was going on? There were indeed dead trees in the German forests in the late 1970s and early 1980s, but they had died for "conventional" reasons of various known tree diseases and problems with the soil, some related to unusually harsh winters at the time. But there was apparently a strong "demand" for a theory that could offer a universal explanation based on an ever increasing "pollution" caused by an unsustainable industrialization. This was about ten years after the publication of *The Limits to Growth*, so the ground had been prepared. *Our Common Future* mentions forest death caused by acid rain. By the early 1990s the forest death hypothesis had been discredited and retracted by its initiators. Experiments on trees, both in the United States and in Europe, found no relationship between acid rain and tree disease.[15] Nevertheless, the disappearance of the forest death hypothesis from the media was quieter than its entrance had been.[16]

And what happened to acid rain? Even if its effect on forests was grossly exaggerated, it was by no means a positive contribution to the environment, and sulfur emissions have been known as a local health hazard for a long time. The industrialized countries of the world made a conscious effort to reduce sulfur emissions from fossil fuels, in particular from coal-fired power stations. Limits were imposed on how much sulfur each power plant could emit. In the United States emission allowances became tradable, ensuring that emissions would be reduced in the cheapest possible way.[17] After having increased exponentially from 1950 to the early 1970s, the emissions of sulfur from burning fossil fuels have declined worldwide, and in the "old" industrialized world they have declined by 80–90 percent since the early 1970s.[18]

The forest death story illustrates two things. First, environmental problems can be dealt with by technology and economics when the benefits are perceived as outweighing the costs. Second, media and politics can distort perceptions of such problems way out of proportion to their degree of seriousness. Unproven hypotheses can be sold as scientific "truth" if this appeals to the public's perceptions about what the world is like, no matter how ill founded. World saviors of various kinds are quick to appeal to a "scientific consensus" when there is none such and quick to produce such "consensus" as best they can by ostracizing and silencing those who hold a different opinion. The forest death story serves as a warning example of what could be going on, and probably is going on, with respect to the debate on global warming.

THE OZONE LAYER

I round off this chapter with a few words on the ozone layer and the phasing out of chlorofluorocarbon gases. These gases became widespread as coolants in refrigerators and drivers in spray cans of various kinds. Released from spray cans, these gases, apparently harmless to humans, dissipate into the atmosphere, as they also do ultimately from refrigerators when the equipment is scrapped.

In the early 1970s, two American scientists discovered that these gases could harm the ozone layer in the stratosphere. The ozone layer filters out ultraviolet rays so its breakdown could cause skin cancers and other harmful effects for life on earth. These results were originally dismissed by the chemical industry, but when a thinning of the ozone layer over Antarctica (the ozone hole) was discovered by British scientists in the 1980s the issue became urgent. International meetings were called and fairly soon resulted in the Montreal Protocol of 1987, which mandates the phasing out of chlorofluorocarbon gases. Originally this applied to the rich countries of the world only, with the poor countries being phased in later. The Montreal Protocol has been uniquely successful in that it has been universally ratified by the countries of the world. It has also been successful in the sense that the emissions of the said gases have diminished and the ozone hole problem apparently has not gotten any worse. The ozone hole appears over Antarctica in the southern spring; the largest hole so far appeared in 2006. The ozone-depleting substances remain in the stratosphere for decades, so any effect on the ozone hole would be gradual despite falling emissions; an immediate dramatic reduction is not to be expected.[19]

The Montreal Protocol was a model for the Kyoto Protocol in crucial ways, one of them being that the rich countries were supposed to be the first to take action, with the poor countries being phased in later. But the fate of the two protocols could hardly be more different. The Kyoto Protocol lapsed in 2012, with nothing to replace it but promises to take some action by 2015, promises that are likely to turn out empty. The Kyoto Protocol has had a minimal effect on the concentration of carbon dioxide in the atmosphere, which has continued to increase at an undiminished rate.

Why these widely different outcomes? The greenhouse gas problem is vastly more complicated than the problem with chlorofluorocarbon gases. First there is the effect. The effect of greenhouse gases on the climate is disputed, and the effects of a changed climate on human living conditions and activities are highly uncertain and of both negative and positive kind. The effect of thinning the ozone layer is uniquely bad, even if its strength can be disputed. And there are those who on scientific grounds question the importance and even the entire role of chlorofluorocarbon gases as destroyers of atmospheric ozone.[20]

Secondly, the potential losses from phasing out chlorofluorocarbon gases were nowhere near the potential losses from phasing out carbon dioxide emissions. Our critical dependence on fossil fuels and the dearth of credible substitutes have already been discussed. There were substitutes available for chlorofluorocarbon gases so they could be phased out relatively easily, even if the substitutes (hydrofluorocarbons) have their own problems, being highly potent greenhouse gases. It helped that only twelve countries emitted 78 percent of chlorofluorocarbon gases at the time the Montreal Protocol was agreed, with the United States a leading producer.[21]

NOTES

1. Sondergaard (2009), p. 49.
2. Quoted in an epigraph to and on page 66 in Michaels and Balling (2009).
3. See, for example, Singer and Avery (2007), Michaels and Balling (2009), Idso, Carter, and Singer (2011), and various papers by MIT meteorologist Richard Lindzen.
4. Quoted from Idso, Carter, and Singer (eds., 2011), p. vi.
5. Op-ed in the *New York Times*, June 1, 2013.
6. Numbers 31.

7. Ridley (2010), p. 138.

8. See Ridley (2010), p. 125.

9. See IPCC Fourth Assessment Report, *Climate Change 2007: Impacts, Adaptation and Vulnerability*, chapter 5 and table 5.7, p. 301.

10. See Executive Summary, p. xi. This is a comprehensive report on the economics of climate change, commissioned by the British government and led by Nicholas Stern. The report was published in 2006.

11. See Sondergaard (2009), pp. 126–27.

12. The story of the forest death mania has been told in several places. One is *Chronik einer Panik* by Günter Keil, *Die Zeit*, December 9, 2004. See also *Waldsterben in the Forests of Central Europe and Eastern North America: Fantasy or Reality?* by John M. Skelly and John L. Innes, *Plant Disease*, Vol. 78, No. 11, 1994, pp. 1021–32.

13. The story is told in Ridley (2010), p. 305.

14. See the preface to Michaels and Balling (2009).

15. See Lomborg (2001), chapter 16, and Bolch and Lyons (1993), pp. 97–100.

16. According to Keil (op.cit.), only 4 of 54 daily papers in Germany reported the retraction of the forest death hypothesis by its instigator.

17. See Richard Schmalensee and others: *An Interim Evaluation of Sulfur Dioxide Emissions Trading* in *Journal of Economic Perspectives*, Vol. 12, 1998, pp. 53–68.

18. On global emissions, see S. J. Smith et al.: *Anthropogenic sulfur dioxide emissions 1950–2005* in *Atmospheric Chemistry and Physics*, Vol. 11, 2011, pp. 1101–16.

19. On this, see "Scientific Assessment of Ozone Depletion 2010," World Meteorological Organization, Global Ozone Research and Monitoring Project—Report, No. 52.

20. See Bolch and Lyons (1993), chapter 7.

21. See Haq and Paul (2012).

Chapter Seven

Is the World Overpopulated?

[Preventive check on population increase] is peculiar to man, and arises from that distinctive superiority in his reasoning faculties, which enables him to calculate distant consequences.

—The Reverend Thomas Malthus, *An Essay on the Principles of Population* (1999/1798), p. 9

It is certain that modern agriculture and modern public health, indeed, modern civilization, could not exist without an unrelenting war against the return of a true balance of nature.

—Ira L. Baldwin (biologist), *Science*
Vol. 137, No. 3535 (1962), pp. 1042–43

Worries that the world will not be able to feed itself have been with us for a long time. The most famous exponent of such ideas is probably Thomas Malthus, who in 1798 published his *Essay on the Principles of Population*. He argued that mankind is capable of multiplying its numbers geometrically, while agricultural production can only increase arithmetically. Mankind was therefore destined to subsist at a level close to what the earth could support; population growth generated by abnormally good times would be self-correcting through famine in worse times. There is little doubt that this was a good description of the world as it had been up to his time, but subsequently he was proven as wrong as anyone could be. The reasons? Food production proved capable of rising much faster than population, and population increase together with economic growth apparently has some built-in stabilizers that over time reduce population growth. Yet we would do well to recognize that at some point there is a limit to how much food for humans the planet can produce. But we have little idea of what it is, and it has in modern times been steadily pushed outwards by technological progress. Are we just fortuitous that we have not yet reached it? Can we rely on countervailing forces to reduce population growth in a timely fashion so that the limit will never be reached? We do not know.

Nevertheless, there is a number of prophets predicting a looming disaster from uncontrolled population growth. Some have burned their fingers badly with their predictions. One of them is professor Paul Ehrlich of Stanford University. In the prologue to his famous book *The Population Bomb*, published in 1968, he sets out as follows:

> The battle to feed all of humanity is over. In the 1970s and the 1980s hundreds of millions of people will starve to death in spite of any crash programs embarked upon now. At this late date nothing can prevent a substantial increase in the world death rate, although many lives could be saved through dramatic programs to "stretch" the carrying capacity of the earth by increasing food production and providing for more equitable distribution of whatever food is available. But these programs will only provide a stay of execution unless they are accompanied by determined and successful efforts at population control.

That "stay of execution" has now lasted for quite a while. True, millions, but probably not hundreds of millions, have died of starvation since *The Population Bomb* was written. They died because of local disasters which relief agencies could not cope with in a timely fashion and because of general economic underdevelopment of their countries making it impossible to help them with domestically produced food, but they did not die because the food production capacity of the planet had been exceeded. Over these two decades, food production kept pace with population increase, and from 1970 to 1990 world population increased from 3.7 billion to 5.3 billion. Undeterred by this, in 1991 came a new book by Ehrlich, this time with his wife as co-author. The book was entitled *The Population Explosion*. One might think that what was an undetonated bomb in 1968 had exploded in the meantime, but it was probably just a need for a different title. On page 17 we read "[w]e shouldn't delude ourselves: the population explosion will come to an end before very long." Well, we shall see. Further twenty years have gone by.

In 2009 Paul Ehrlich was given the opportunity to revisit *The Population Bomb*.[1] He was unrepentant. Some formulations were, with hindsight, unfortunate and overblown. That notwithstanding, "[P]erhaps the most serious flaw in 'The Bomb' was that it was much too optimistic about the future." How so? It "alerted people to the importance of environmental issues." After its publication, global warming and its alleged perils came on the agenda, and worries about other environmental problems became more prominent.

So "The Bomb" was right for the wrong reasons. An interesting argument. Nostradamus would probably agree.

Time has, in general, not been kind to Paul and Anne Ehrlich's prophesies. Here are excerpts from another book (*The End of Affluence*). "We are facing, within the next three decades, the disintegration of an unstable world of nation-states infected with growthmania. The game of unlimited growth is ending, like it or not" (page 4). And several pages further on (page 34): "What you need to know is that in ten or fifteen years—twenty or twenty-five at most—you will be living in a world *extremely different* from that of today—one that. . . will prove extremely unpleasant" (italics in the original). That sounds frightening, until one takes a look at the cover and notices the publication year—1974. Paul and Anne Ehrlich's books get better and better over time, albeit in ways they might not like. As already noted, a golden rule for Doomsday prophets is never to make predictions that can be falsified in their lifetime.

Figure 7.1 shows the rates of growth of population and the four most important crops in the world since 1960.[2] The first thing to notice is that over this period the growth rates of all four crops have outstripped the growth in world population. This is a manifestation of the simple fact that the world of the early twenty-first century is not any nearer to the limits of feeding itself than it was in 1960, despite the fact that world population has more than doubled in the meantime (three billion in 1960, 6.9 in 2010).

How is this possible? There was a lot of unused agricultural land back in 1960, and there still is. That is one reason. But the main reason why the

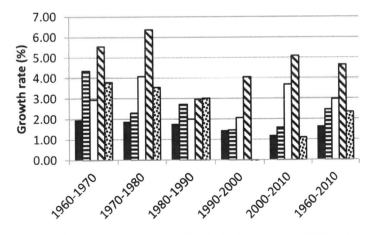

■ Population ⊟ Rice ☐ Corn (maize) ◩ Soybeans ⊠ Wheat

Figure 7.1. Population growth and production growth of the world's most important crops. Source: calculated from data from the FAO and the World Bank.

food production could keep pace with this formidable population growth is technological progress, in particular the so-called green revolution, of which more below.

Yet the pessimist can find something to worry about; the growth rate for wheat and rice has declined. But so has the rate of population growth; it is not inevitable that population growth will necessarily outpace the growth in food production. The only bad story we have is the zero growth rate for wheat in the decade 1990–2000, but this is due to a bumper crop in 1990 and a mediocre one in 2000.

As we can see from Figure 7.1 the population growth has fallen decade by decade since the 1960s; if the trend since 1980 persists the growth rate will have fallen to zero by the mid-2050s, with world population about 8.5 billion. Will it? Possibly, and particularly if world economic growth continues and spreads to the still poor countries of the world, contrary to the sayings of prophets lamenting "growthmania." Will there be enough food for 8.5 billion people? Hopefully, and especially if we take advantage of the potential of genetic technology, the green revolution of our time.

WHY DOES POPULATION GROWTH FALL?

Population growth is determined by the difference between births and deaths. The enormous growth of world population since the industrial revolution depends primarily on a falling death rate; the birth rate has fallen in virtually all societies, but the death rate has fallen even more. The fall in the death rate is due to a host of factors; not just better medicines and health care but also better nutrition, housing, and other material conditions. So if we are worried about population growth, we have the recipe how to control it.

Except for the one-child policy in China, no society has attempted to control the birth rate. This is still the outcome of individual decisions, which needless to say are influenced by policy measures such as public child care, economic support to having children, etc. That in turn makes population growth the outcome of individual decisions which we can be sure take little or no account of what the ability of the planet is to support a growing population. Hence, whether or not world population turns out to stay within the limits of the globe to support it will depend on whether or not the outcome of these individual and uncoordinated decisions turn out to be fortuitous, but not on any deliberate central planning based on an objective assessment of the planet's carrying capacity.

But before we begin to worry over the apparent risk that population growth might exceed the world's capacity to feed itself we would do well to consider whether there might exist self-correcting feedback mechanisms that would prevent this from happening. It appears that this might be case. As Figure 7.1 shows, the growth rate of the world population has fallen substantially since the 1960s. In 1960 there were three billion people in the world. Over the next decade world population grew at an annualized rate of almost 2 percent. If it had continued to grow at that rate, there would have been eight billion people in the world by 2010, but there were less than seven. In the meantime the growth rate had fallen, and it was only 1.2 percent in the first decade of this century.

This reduction in population growth is associated with an increase in income and standard of living, so it is tempting to conclude that economic growth would be the most potent instrument in limiting population growth. Figure 7.2 shows population growth rates for low income, middle income, and high income countries. The high income countries have the lowest growth rate, despite having the best medical services and the best nutrition and shelter. Both in high income and middle income countries the population growth rate has fallen uniformly since the 1960s. As to low income countries, not only do they have the highest population growth rate, but it was also rising until 1990. Since then it has come down, but is still twice as high as in middle income countries and three times higher than in high income countries.

Viewed from a different angle, the reason why the population growth rate has fallen is that many countries have been in what is called a demographic transition. First the death rate falls, because of better health and nutrition and other factors, and then after some time the birth rate falls as well. In the meantime, while the gap between the birth rate and the death rate is widening, population growth is high and rising. Countries have gone through the demographic tran-

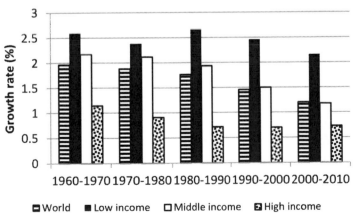

Figure 7.2. **Rate of population growth. Calculated from World Bank data.**

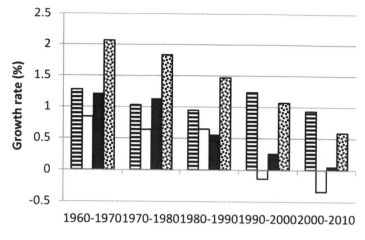

Figure 7.3. Rate of population growth in selected countries. Calculated from World Bank data.

sition at different times, rich countries earlier than the poorer ones. The poor countries of the world are now typically approaching the end of this transition. In the words of a UN consultant, "it's not that people suddenly started breeding like rabbits, it's just that they stopped dying like flies."[3]

Figure 7.3 shows the population growth rate in selected countries. The Chinese population growth rate has dropped decade by decade, from more than 2 percent in the 1960s to 0.6 percent in the first decade of this century. In Japan the growth rate has fallen since 1980 and is now close to zero. In the United States the growth rate has not fallen much since 1960 and actually increased in the 1990s, but the United States receives substantial immigration. In Russia the population growth rate turned negative after 1990. The economic turmoil after the collapse of the Soviet Union meant falling standards of living and increased uncertainty for a large part, perhaps the majority, of the population and led to a substantial decline in expected lifetime.

What, then, lies behind the apparent paradox that population growth is highest in poor countries, the very ones where health care, shelter, and nutrition are poorest and the death rates also are highest? One is the already mentioned demographic transition, which occurred later in the poor countries than the rich ones. Otherwise the causes are no doubt complex and different from one country to another, but some are likely to be common to all. First, there is the security of old age (which in poor countries is not necessarily very old). This was traditionally provided by having an offspring able to provide for aging parents. In a society with a high death rate, especially for children, there was a risk that none of very few children would survive. Furthermore, the governments of poor countries are in no position to provide care for the aged in general. In the modern welfare state health care and care for the aged is no longer provided by the family but has been universalized and impersonalized and thereby removed one major motive for having children. Needless to say, the welfare state requires a certain degree of affluence well above what the poor countries of the world can provide. Affluence itself probably reduces the motivation for having children, as people seem to become more self-centered and fixated on their own careers and self-indulgence as they become richer. Then there is the emancipation of women, historically associated with a growing affluence; as women acquire a career outside the home child care gets in the way and interferes with the pursuit of an independent career. Lastly there is prevention technology, which poor people cannot afford. All of this implies that the birth rate is likely to fall as societies get richer.

One may wonder whom Paul Ehrlich and his crowd are trying to advise. His books are unlikely to be read by the poor or even by decision makers in poor countries, the very ones that are growing fastest. They are most likely to be read by academics and decision makers in rich countries, but that is where the problem is least pressing or not pressing at all. The only useful impact might be on agencies and politicians involved with foreign aid, who might be persuaded to press for contraception and family planning in the poor countries they are trying to help. That is fine, but the greatest help is probably coming from general economic growth in the poor countries of the world, if the experience of those already rich is anything to go by.

Nevertheless, economic growth in the poor countries of the world does pose some problems for food production. As people get rich they want to eat better. As incomes have risen in China, people have demanded more luxurious food items such as beef. As a result, China's import of cattle meat increased more than fourfold from 1989 to 2010.[4] The import of soymeal, an important feed component, was still well below 10 million tonnes in 1999 but was 57 million tonnes in 2010. The problem with this is that feeding people with meat, especially beef, takes up very much more land and requires more water than feeding them with cereals. While economic growth is likely to reduce population growth it will increase the demand for land and water to grow food, just because people will demand a more luxurious diet.

THE GREEN REVOLUTION

In the 1950s and 1960s it was conventional wisdom that India would never be able to feed itself, being entrapped in a truly Malthusian dilemma; the mismatch between a growing population and stagnant food production would doom India to a permanent poverty trap with recurrent famines.[5] There were some good reasons to believe this. In his book *Seeds of Change* Lester Brown describes how India and Pakistan were being fed by food aid from the United States; for "several years in the 1960s, U.S. food aid was feeding an estimated 100 million people a year." This was not likely to be sustainable; at some point either the surplus land in the United States or the willingness of the American government to buy surplus food and give it away to foreign countries would come to an end.

What changed all this was the green revolution, seeds of wheat (relevant for India), corn (maize), and rice that could produce much larger harvests than traditional seeds. Lester Brown describes very eloquently in his book how revolutionary the transition to new seeds was in Southeast Asia; over just a few years the land under the new crops multiplied many times over. Figures 7.4 and 7.5 illustrate the implications for India. Wheat production has increased handsomely, both in India and the world, since 1961; in India the increase began in the late 1960s, after the green revolution took hold. Until the late 1970s India imported wheat every single year, but since then India has exported wheat in some years, and for several years in the beginning of this century these exports were quite formidable.

The green revolution has by now run its course. The miracle seeds developed by Norman Borlaug and others in the 1960s have been planted where they will grow and revolutionized the world supply of food. But there is a green revolution of our time, the genetic engineering that makes it possible for plants to resist pests and for animals to grow faster. Unfortunately, this technology has been hit by the warped philosophy of environmentalism. Genetic engineering is seen as a way of "playing god." Because of the "nature knows best" mind-set

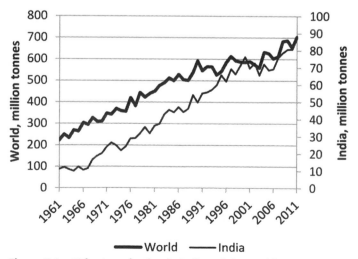

Figure 7.4. Wheat production in India and the world. Source: FAO.

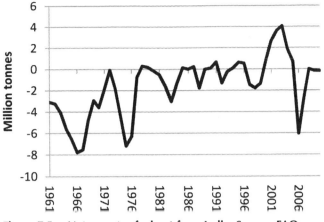

Figure 7.5.   Net exports of wheat from India. Source: FAO.

it is seen as evil, as it interferes with nature. The slogan of "Frankenstein food" has caught on. The precautionary principle is, needless to say, invoked as an argument against allowing genetically modified seeds or other living organisms. One can never know. . . . Even if harmful effects of genetically modified food can neither be presumed nor proven it is nevertheless banned.[6]

The resistance against genetically modified organisms varies from place to place. In many underdeveloped countries they have been enthusiastically welcomed. These countries are the ones with the most pressing need for more food. Much of the grain harvest in the United States comes from genetically modified seeds and has done so for years. No health problems have emerged. In Europe, on the other hand, genetically modified organisms are generally outlawed; only two crops, insect-resistant corn (maize) and potatoes for industrial use have been permitted.[7] By 2009, no less than 10 percent of all arable land in the world was planted with genetically modified crops.[8] Scientists supporting genetic engineering point out that it is not fundamentally different from selective breeding and breeding across species, only faster and more precise.[9]

But also in the United States there is resistance against genetically modified organisms; in 2011 the Food and Drug Administration was considering an application to approve genetically modified salmon, alleged to grow twice as fast as ordinary farmed salmon. Senators from—you guessed it—three American salmon fishing states (Alaska, Washington, and Oregon) got together for an initiative to prevent the Food and Drug Administration from using its funds to even study this case. "We don't need Frankenfish" they were quoted as saying. In the EU, decisions about whether or not to allow genetically modified organisms are taken at the political level, but rather than pandering to special interests the European politicians seem to be dancing to the environmentalists' tune. Some crops have been banned outright, others have been under study for a long time. One of the latter is genetically modified soya, which has been under study since 2005. This hit Romania hard when she became a member of the EU in 2007. From 1999 Romania had been cultivating genetically modified soya, and in 2006 it amounted to almost 70 percent of all soya planted in the country. It was considered the most profitable crop in Romania, due to higher yields and lower herbicide costs than conventional soya. But upon becoming a member of the EU Romania had to quit her cultivation of genetically modified soya.

Environmentalist opponents of genetic modifications of plants would do well to ponder the following. Some genetic modifications increase natural resistance to pests, reducing the need for pesticides. Other modifications enhance the capacity to absorb nutrition from fertilizers, reducing the need for fertilizers and their environmental side effects. These and other genetic modifications increase crop yield and thus reduce the need for land to be put under the plow. This in turn would increase land that can be preserved as wild nature without compromising necessary food production. Then there are modifications which would increase the nutritional value of crops by enhancing their contents of micronutrients such as vitamins and iron.[10] Even from an environmentalist standpoint, genetic modification need not be all bad. Only the fundamentalist's world is neatly divided between good and evil and then only after putting some blinds on.

NOTES

1. In the *Electronic Journal of Sustainable Development*, Summer 2009. www.ejsd.org.

2. Sources: World Bank (population) and FAO (crops). The FAO-data begin in 1961, so the first decade is 1961–1970 and the 50 years period is 1961–2011 for the crops.

3. Quoted in Miller (1998), p. 293.

4. FAO statistical database (FAOSTAT).

5. But there were contrary views. In his book *Asian Drama*, Gunnar Myrdal noted the extremely low output of food grains per acre and concluded that it must be possible to increase output through better practices and at relatively low cost (Myrdal, 1968, p. 1251).

6. Some of the shenanigans of the organized opposition to genetic engineering are described in Miller (1997), pp. 43–51.

7. EuropaBio, The European Association for Bioindustries, 2010.

8. *Sustainable Food Consumption and Production in a Resource-Constrained World*. European Commission—Standing committee on agricultural research, February 2010, p. 80.

9. See Miller (1997), especially pp. 12–16 and 22–27.

10. Goklany (2001) lists a number of advantages of genetically modified crops and weighs arguments for and against their use.

Chapter Eight

Fisheries, Aquaculture, and the Oceans

In the late 1860s, New England fishermen rose up in protest against net fishermen. They deluged the legislatures of Connecticut, Massachusetts, and Rhode Island with petitions. . . . The head of the U.S. Fish Commission concluded that netters were about to wipe out entire species. Despite the fact that the netting continued, the species came back in abundance. The protests had begun during a natural crash in fish populations. They faded out with the new population boom.

—Kaufman (1994), pp. 99–100

Unless humans act now, seafood may disappear by 2048, concludes the lead author of a new study that paints a grim picture for ocean and human health.

—National Geographic News, November 2, 2006, reporting on a study by Boris Worm and others

"Fisheries are collapsing throughout the world," says one publication.[1] The notion is widespread. A story is told of a British fisheries scientist who was being knighted. At the ceremony the queen came around to him and asked what he did. "I'm a fisheries scientist, Madam." "Does that mean that you count the fish?" "Yes, Madam." "There aren't as many of them around as there used to be, are there?" said the queen and moved on to the next, without waiting for an answer.

There may not be as many of them around as there used to be, but yet when one looks at the overall picture the much touted depletion of the world's fish stocks does not stare one in the face. Figure 8.1 shows the world fish production since 1950. The difference between total production and the production in the capture fisheries is due to aquaculture, which will be further discussed

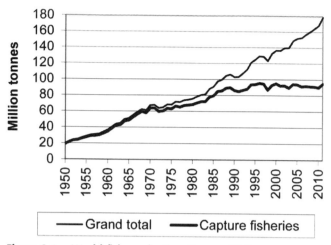

Figure 8.1. World fish production. Source: FAO.

below, but the situation in the capture fisheries is what the notion of the overexploited oceans is about. We see that the catches in the capture fisheries increased rapidly up to about 1970, and again in the 1980s, but since the late 1980s they have fluctuated without much trend. So what one sees is stagnation, but not depletion. We seem to have come to the end of the road as far as capturing wild fish from the sea is concerned. This is bad news, as the world population is still growing and the need for more food rising, but it is not the catastrophe one could be led to believe is taking place, judging from some reports in the media.

Behind the overall picture provided by aggregate catches there are stories of terrible failures, however. Some fish stocks have been depleted. Some of them have recovered, but not all. These stories are instructive. They illustrate how difficult it is to forecast the outcomes of processes of which we have no previous experience and very limited information about anyway—in this case rapidly intensified exploitation of fish stocks which are strongly affected by environmental forces about which we know very little. The point can be made that "management failures" are unavoidable stepping stones in learning about the consequences of overexploitation and even finding out what the limits of sustainable exploitation are. Under these circumstances the "precautionary principle" is something of an oxymoron. Even more importantly, these examples show how mistakes—which were probably unavoidable given the state of knowledge at the time—became lessons learned and led to improvement and avoidance of similar mistakes being repeated.

The collapse of the California sardine was probably the first major fishery collapse in the world. Figure 8.2 shows the landings of Pacific sardine

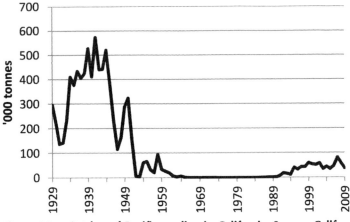

Figure 8.2. Catches of Pacific sardine in California. Source: California commercial catches database.

in California. The landings from this fishery were more than half a million tonnes in the 1930s and early 1940s. At that time there was a large canning industry and a fish meal industry in California based on the sardine. Both of these disappeared in the 1950s as the sardine landings dwindled. In 1967 the sardine fishery was closed down, and it took more than two decades for the sardine stock to recover. In the late 1980s the sardine fishery was opened again, but the landings have been nowhere near their historical levels since, as there are now tight limits on sardine landings. Partly the reason is a desire to avoid another collapse of the stock, but on top of that the old canning and meal industries are now gone and the demand for sardines is less; the landings are now used for bait or for export to Australia and other countries as feed for farmed tuna.

It used to be believed that the collapse of the sardine stock was due to mismanagement; to a failure to set a limit to sardine landings commensurate with what the stock could support. Later it was realized that a change in oceanographic conditions could have played a role: In the 1940s the temperature in the sea off California fell, which was harmful for the sardine. Sediments from the ocean bottom outside Santa Barbara indicate that sardine and anchovy have alternated over time long before they were fished on any significant scale, probably due to fluctuations in ocean climate.[2]

The collapse of the sardine fishery in California led to the development of fish meal industries in other parts of the world, in particular in South Africa and Peru. Some of the equipment idled by the sardine collapse was sold to these countries. The anchovy fishery in Peru developed rapidly; from virtually nothing in the mid-1950s to the world's largest fishery, with

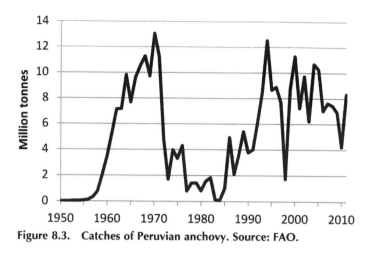

Figure 8.3.   Catches of Peruvian anchovy. Source: FAO.

12 million tonnes landed in 1971. And then another collapse; in 1973 the anchovy landings in Peru fell below two million tonnes and took over ten years to recover (Figure 8.3).

What precipitated the collapse of the anchovy fishery in Peru was a strong El Niño. With hindsight, the fishery was not restrained in a timely enough manner when the El Niño arrived. By contrast, the strong El Niño of 1997–1998 had only a transient effect on the Peruvian anchovy fishery. It declined to almost nothing in the 1998 season, but recovered to its earlier level in 1999. It is tempting to conclude that the experience of 1973 taught the Peruvians a lesson and led them to manage their anchovy more carefully next time a serious El Niño arrived. That lesson is apparently lost on some. The aquarium in Monterey, California, known for its "advice" on what fish it is environmentally safe to eat, shows a diagram of the catches of Peruvian anchovy as an example of how overfishing is depleting the world's oceans. The diagram ends in 1984, just prior to the recovery. In July 2002 the diagram had not yet been updated. A good story should not be ruined by facts.

A few years before the collapse of the Peruvian anchovy fishery, several herring stocks in the North Atlantic collapsed. The largest of these was the Norwegian spring-spawning herring (Figure 8.4). In the early 1960s there was a technological revolution in the herring fishery; the nets and the boats became bigger and more effective, and new fish finding equipment made it easier to locate the herring shoals. The catches increased rapidly, but at the same time the herring stock was declining fast due to disadvantageous oceanographic conditions. The stock was in the process of literally being wiped out when the fishery was stopped in the early 1970s.

It took almost 20 years for the stock to recover. Since that time the herring fishery has been managed by fish quotas which the stock has been able

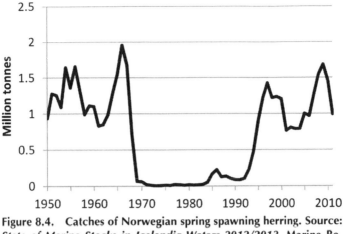

Figure 8.4. Catches of Norwegian spring spawning herring. Source: *State of Marine Stocks in Icelandic Waters 2012/2013*, Marine Research Institute, Reykjavík, 2013, Table 3.21.6.

to support. This new management regime has not been without problems; the herring stock migrates between the economic zones of several countries and is also at times accessible in international waters outside the jurisdiction of any country. This means that the countries utilizing the stock have to agree on setting and enforcing limits on the total catches of herring. These agreements have been thwarted at times by the variable migration path of the herring stock. No country will agree to a herring quota unless it thinks it will do as well as it would on its own in the absence of any agreement. If the Icelanders believe that a lot of herring is coming their way, they will not accept a small herring quota.

There are strong reasons to believe that the herring collapse of the late 1960s was unavoidable and a necessary if costly learning experience. It used to be difficult to locate herring shoals; this was done either by dropping a line with a sinker and observing or feeling how it was dislocated by dense shoals underneath, or by observing ripples on the water. Encircling them was accomplished with small boats—rowboats in the old days and later equipped with engines—and hauling them in was done by hand. Fish finding equipment and mechanical winches revolutionized the fishery over just a few years in the 1960s. The most advanced fish finding equipment first made its appearance on the research vessels, and in those days the fishery scientists took pride in finding the fish and telling the fishermen where it was. For this they were popular, but their popularity among the fishermen waned as the scientists realized that the herring was being overexploited and that the catches had to be severely curtailed. It took some time for the scientists to realize what was going on; the technological revolution was very rapid, and some signals of overexploitation, such as declining catches per boat, were not very strong. There was also some disagreement among scientists on whether the stock was being overexploited and to what degree.

Even if the depletion of the herring stock had been realized in a timely enough fashion, the required cutback in catches would surely have been made difficult and probably impossible to attain because of the absence of coastal state jurisdiction at sea. In 1970, at the time of the herring collapse, coastal state jurisdiction over fisheries was still only 12 nautical miles. Much of the herring fishery took place outside 12 miles, and the stock migrated seasonally between the waters of different sovereign states. Fishing fleets from several nations were engaged in the fishery, with Norway, Iceland, and the Soviet Union being the most important. At least those three, and probably some of the minor players as well, would have had to agree on limiting their catches and enforce those limits to save the herring stock. This did not happen, and it appears that at the time there was limited understanding that any restraint was needed. As the stock dwindled it ceased migrating as widely as it used to and became confined to the Norwegian economic zone, which in 1977 was extended to 200 nautical miles. In the end Norway banned all further catches of herring, and that ban was in place until 1985. This may possibly have saved the herring stock from oblivion.

Since the herring stock recovered, it has been managed by an overall catch limit, with the total permitted catch divided among the countries involved in the herring fishery. The overall catch quota is set for one year at a time, on the basis of assessment of the herring stock and with a view to its future development. From Figure 8.4 we may note that the annual catch since the recovery in the 1980s has fluctuated considerably. The reason is the variability in the stock size, caused by variability in the ocean environment. This illustrates a point made in chapter 3; sustainable fish catches are likely to mean year-to-year variability. The decline we see in recent years is unlikely to mean another slide toward near-depletion, and preliminary figures for recent years do not bear that out. This is also illustrated by the Peruvian anchovy (Figure 8.3) after the recovery, where the year-to-year variations in landings are even greater.

The establishment of the 200-mile economic zone is itself an example of how human institutions develop in response to changing technology and other challenges. Fish stocks used to be open access resources; that is, anyone could go and fish on the high seas, the area outside national jurisdiction. Traditionally national jurisdiction covered only a narrow belt along the coast; the British Empire in its heyday came close to getting three nautical miles from the low water mark accepted as an international rule. As long as fishing technology was primitive enough for fishing not to make too much of an impact on the fish stocks this was entirely adequate, but as technology developed this spelled disaster. With no limits on access to fish stocks, technological progress in fisheries is ultimately counterproductive, leading to depletion of stocks and declining catches of fish. As factory trawlers were developed in the 1960s, many coastal states became worried that these highly efficient fleets would mop up the fish stocks off their shores and pushed for extended fisheries jurisdiction at sea. This came to fruition when the third UN conference on the law of the sea endorsed the idea of a 200-mile exclusive economic zone in the 1970s, and many countries established such zones in the late 1970s. In some cases the exclusive economic zone enclosed fish stocks within the jurisdiction of a single state and thus made it possible for that state to limit the catches to whatever suits its interests, which typically means preserving a stock to provide sustainable catches. In other cases fish stocks migrate between the jurisdictions of two or more states so that the states have to agree on any effective catch limitation, and in yet other cases stocks may still be accessible outside the jurisdiction of any state, which makes for some thorny management problems.

Even if it is highly likely, to say the least, that the 200-mile exclusive economic zone has promoted the preservation of fish stocks, there is at least one serious counterexample. The northern cod of Newfoundland used to be one of the largest cod stocks in the North Atlantic. It was also one of the stocks perceived to be under threat from the factory trawlers that were developed in the 1960s. Figure 8.5 shows the catches of cod from this stock from 1850 to 1992. The high peak in the 1960s is due to the arrival of factory trawlers on the banks of Newfoundland. After Canada established its 200-mile zone in 1977 foreign fleets were banned from the Canadian zone, and the Canadian

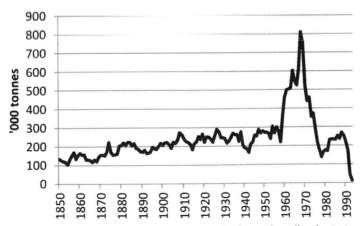

Figure 8.5. Catches of the northern cod of Newfoundland 1850–1993. Source: Ransom Meyers.

federal government announced a cautious management policy aimed at limiting fish catches to what was sustainable, trying to err on the conservative side. Despite these intentions, the stock was depleted almost entirely, and it has been under moratorium since 1992, except for some small-scale exploratory fishing. While it is true that foreign fishing fleets had access to the stock outside the Canadian 200-mile zone, this is unlikely to have been decisive. It appears that the Canadian scientists were grossly mistaken in their assessment of the size of the stock and that the authorities hesitated for too long in curtailing the fishery because of the impact on the economy of Newfoundland.

With the caveat that proving the counterfactual is impossible, the establishment of the 200-mile exclusive economic zone was a watershed in fisheries management worldwide. Conservation is essentially about deferring benefits over time; the reason why we do not take all the fish we can lay our hands on today is the knowledge that nothing would then be available tomorrow. But for such deferment to make any sense one must be reasonably sure to be able to get the benefits from whatever fish left today for growth and reproduction. That was the missing element in the old regime of freedom of fishing wherever and whenever one liked. The individual fisherman has little or no incentive to leave any fish that might later be caught by someone else, or the offspring of which might be caught by someone else. The same applies to individual countries sharing a fish stock; Iceland is not going to spare any mackerel in its zone if it is mainly for the benefit of Scots and Norwegians. It is presumably easier for the fisheries administrators of a handful of countries to agree on limits to fish catches than it would be, say, for a thousand fishermen, possibly from different countries, but then the countries involved must be reasonably sure that the agreements they conclude cannot be upended by outsiders who could access the fish. This is why many of the unsolved fisheries management problems occur for fish stocks accessible on the high seas, that is, outside the 200-mile exclusive economic zones. The UN Law of the Sea Convention explicitly recognizes the right of any state to fish on the high seas. This makes it difficult if not impossible to limit fishing in this area.

Unfortunately the countries of the world have not taken the logical and necessary step to further extend the economic zones of individual countries and close off what remains of the high seas. It was in the wake of the establishment of the 200-mile zone that countries began to agree on effective limits on fish catches, and it was the national jurisdiction within the 200-mile zone that made it possible to enforce such agreements. On the high seas it is up to the state where the fishing boats are registered to enforce rules and regulations over them. Some states are uninterested or unable to do so, which is why they have become flag states of convenience for boat owners that wish to circumvent fisheries regulations.

THE STATUS OF THE WORLD'S FISH STOCKS

The FAO (Food and Agricultural Organization of the United Nations) issues a biennial report entitled *The Status of World's Fisheries and Aquaculture*. This is probably the most authoritative source on the issue and one that is often quoted. The way it is quoted can be quite revealing for the mind-set of those who do so; a frequent formulation is "85 percent of the world's fish stocks are fully utilized or overexploited." Why fully utilized stocks should be bundled together with overexploited stocks is less than clear; one would think that utilizing stocks fully would be a good thing, from the point of view of maximizing food supplies. As of 2009, almost 60 percent of all fish stocks monitored by the FAO were classified as fully exploited while 30 percent were classified as overexploited and 13 percent as not fully exploited.[3]

The FAO is itself fully cognizant of the limitations of this stock survey and admonishes against abusing it. The survey is limited in scope, covering only 10 percent of exploited stocks by number, but 80 percent in terms of landings, mostly in rich countries' waters. This could well mean a brighter picture than it should be, since the rich countries of the world are better equipped to monitor their fish stocks and control their fisheries. Then there is the problem of finding the right benchmark for appropriate exploitation. The fluctuations in the ocean environment make this particularly difficult; a catch that this year may be well within the limits of sustainability could be way too large next year. Fish mortality or exploitation rate are the appropriate measures, but not easy to estimate or control. The statistic pertains to the number of stocks; there is no weighting with respect to size or value, except that the stocks comprised are among the larger ones in world fisheries in terms of quantity. Over time more and more stocks have become covered by the FAO status report.

Looking at the FAO assessment over the period 1974–2009 there is a worrying tendency; the share of overexploited stocks has increased from less than 10 percent to 30.[4] The share of stocks that are fully exploited has hovered around 50 percent, with no trend, but increased suddenly to almost 60 in 2009. Whether this will be sustained remains to be seen. The share of underexploited stocks has decreased from 40 to 13 percent. But there is some distance from a worrying situation to a crisis.

MARINE PROTECTED AREAS

One proposed "solution" to the fisheries problem is to establish so-called marine protected areas where no fishing whatsoever is allowed. Needless to say, this is inspired by environmentalist ideology and has certain similarities to protection of old growth forests where no logging is permitted. The proponents of marine protected areas try occasionally to sell this solution to the fishing industry as a way of improved fisheries management, but this is not easy; the industry is not easily duped into believing that closing off large areas will provide more fish for their boats and money into their coffers. The circumstances under which this could happen are quite special, but not entirely impossible; reefs with sedentary fish could be seeded with juvenile fish from areas closed to fishing, or areas that had been inadvertently depleted could be repopulated with fish from protected areas.

Usually, however, the purpose of marine protected areas is to preserve marine life in its pristine form. The most ambitious proposal at the time of writing concerns a marine protected area in Antarctica, submitted to the Commission for the Conservation of Antarctic Marine Living Resources (CCAMLR).[5] If accepted, this would cover an area of 2.3 million square kilometers; for comparison the Norwegian continental shelf outside the 12-mile territorial limit is slightly more than 2 million square kilometers. While paying lip service to fisheries, the proposal is long on the need to preserve biodiversity and, in particular, wildlife of no commercial use such as penguins, sea birds, and marine mammals. The proposal was discussed at a special meeting of CCAMLR in July 2013, but did not command the necessary consensus for being adopted.

And sometimes the environmentalists do not even bother to pay lip service to the fishing industry and food production. Lately it has become fashionable to campaign against certain types of fishing gear such as long lines and bottom trawls, due to their alleged destruction of marine biodiversity. The marine life on the sea bottom has been compared with the rain forests, and bottom trawls are alleged to destroy this. Sea birds get hooked on long lines when attempting to capture the bait and drown. These effects are supposed to be more important than the contribution of fishing to food production. The affluent and overfed can of course well afford to harbor such sentiments; it happens that icons of the entertainment industry are rolled out in support of these ideas.

AQUACULTURE

From Figure 8.1 we can conclude that the growth in fish production since the late 1980s has come from aquaculture while the capture fisheries have stagnated. This growth in aquaculture has made it possible for fish production to do better than keep pace with population growth and thus do more than its share in contributing to feeding the world. Nevertheless, aquaculture is regarded with suspicion among many environmentalists, who focus on perceived environmental threats of various kinds; pollution of coastal waters because of feed spills; threats to wild fish through the spread of parasites and diseases; and incentives to overfish wild stocks to procure feed.

A curious fact that immediately strikes anyone who examines the feed question is that the production of fish meal has been stagnant for 20 years despite a formidable increase in the production of farmed fish.[6] One reason is that many species of farmed fish do not need feed derived from fish but can be reared on feed from terrestrial plants only. One such is tilapia, a fish the production of which is growing very rapidly. A drawback of such fish is that the positive nutritional values associated with fish stem from fish based feed. A fish, like other organisms, is what it eats.

As to piscivorous (fish eating) fish such as salmon, there are two reasons why the production has increased despite a stagnant production of fish meal. First, much of the world's fish meal production has been diverted from pigs and poultry to production of fish feed.[7] In 1980 only 10 percent of the fish meal produced in the world was used for feeding fish; by 2010 more than a half was used for fish feed. This represents a net gain, from a nutritional point of view. Fish convert a greater percentage of their feed intake to harvestable flesh; fish are cold blooded animals and do not need energy to keep themselves warm like pigs and chicken. There is still some distance left to travel down this path. Fish oil is a more critical factor for a further expansion of the fish farming industry; in 2008 about 85 percent of all fish oil was used in feed blends for fish. The omega-3 fatty acids, cherished because of positive health effects, are derived from the fish oil in the feed mixtures.

A second reason why farming of piscivorous fish has been able to expand despite stagnated production of fish meal is substitution of products from terrestrial plants for fish meal. Even piscivorous fish like salmon get by with less than one-half of the feed being derived from fish meal.[8] Some people believe that a further substitution along these lines could accommodate a further expansion of farming of piscivorous fish. This is probably mistaken. Even if such substitution is technically possible, the ongoing growth in world population and rising incomes leading to increased demand for meat of various kinds will in turn lead to increased demand for terrestrial plants for direct and indirect nutritional purposes other than through fish farming. Added to that is the increased demand for biofuels. Pushing the feed problem onshore is thus unlikely to solve the fish feed problem. Farmers of piscivorous fish would therefore do well by being mentally prepared for approaching the limit to how much can be produced, unless bioengineering comes up with new substitutes for fish meal and oil, such as products derived from algae.

A further argument on the feed issue is that using fish for feed is grossly inefficient; it would be better to use the feed fish for direct human consumption. The problem with this is that there are few if any alternative uses for the feed fish. Fish is a highly perishable commodity, especially in warm climates where much of the raw material for the fish meal industry is procured. This is made worse by the fact that the typical feed fish, such as the Peruvian anchovy, is fatty and deteriorates quickly in a warm climate. It is a costly and technically demanding operation to produce fish products for direct human consumption from fish like that and transport it to the needy in a different part of the world. Only a negligible part of the anchovy catch is presently used for human consumption, for the very simple reason that there is a negligible market for it. Those who might argue that the needy must be supplied irrespective of whether or not they are willing and able to pay for the food should ponder whether it would not make more sense to supply them with cereals that are less demanding in terms of processing, as well as being easier to transport and store. A problem more worthy of their moral indignation is the rising price of cereals due to increased demand for meat and biofuels, which may be putting some foodstuffs out of reach for those least able to pay for it.

The question of feed fish versus food fish is one that markets resolve on their own. In order to make sense of feeding fish with fish, the feed fish must be a lot cheaper than the food fish which it produces. If the feed fish could be used for direct human consumption it is highly likely that it would be too expensive for the fish meal industry. In fact we have seen a major decline in the use of certain types of fish as raw material for fish meal as a result of a development of a consumer market. The bulk of herring and mackerel catches in Norway used to be sold to the fish meal factories. Nowadays most of the catches of these fish goes to direct human consumption, which pays a price that the fish meal factories cannot compete with.

Some environmental organizations, the Monterey Aquarium for example, are on record for maintaining that salmon aquaculture is not sustainable. It is, however, no less sustainable than production of beef. The feed for salmon comes partly from fish meal derived from fish stocks that are managed by fish quotas and in a sustainable way; this has been true for a long time of the Peruvian anchovy, the most important source of fish meal in the world, and of capelin and various other fish. As already stated, the production of fish meal has been fairly constant for 20 years despite a strong increase in production of farmed salmon. The rest comes from plants, mainly soybeans. The reader may ponder the following piece of arithmetic. A beef cow needs 5.75 acres and produces 500 pounds of beef, which would suffice for 1,000 meals. That area could otherwise produce 750 bushels of soybeans, which would produce 26,000 meals of tofu. If the idea is that farmed salmon is not sustainable because it fails to feed the maximum number of people, what should we say of the beef? The environmentalist concern about the sustainability of salmon farming is badly misdirected.

ECOSYSTEM MANAGEMENT

A phrase that for some time has been in vogue is ecosystem-based management of fisheries. At first thought this makes eminent sense. Big fish eat the small fish; one kind of fish feeds on another. Sometimes fish eat their own progeny; supposedly what matters for fish as feed is the size; they eat anything that passes them by and they can get into their mouth. Large cod are known to eat a lot of small cod; fish found in the stomach of a cod have been more than half the predator's size.

As on land, the production in the oceans is driven by sunshine. The phytoplankton converts solar energy into biomass, just as the plants do on land. The zooplankton feeds on the phytoplankton, and fish on the zooplankton. Then come the piscivorous fish that eat smaller fish. Obviously we need to take into account the flow of biomass through this system if we are to utilize it effectively. To utilize the nutritional material as effectively as possible we should eat the phytoplankton, just as we can feed more people on any given piece of land by having them eat plants rather than beef, poultry, or pigs. But capturing the phytoplankton is impossible; the zooplankton is difficult enough. It is possible to capture krill, but it is not known for being particularly tasty. Herring is better, but not all are enthusiastic. There is a certain tendency for fish to be considered better the higher up it is in the food chain; cod more tasty than capelin, salmon better than blue whiting, much like people, up to a point anyway, prefer beef, poultry, and pigs to the plants with which they are fed.

So, in order to utilize the productivity of the ocean intelligently, we need to be able to quantify the flow of biomass through various links in the food chain and to put a price and a cost tag on what we get out of it at each node. One thing that complicates this enormously is that the food chain is an imperfect metaphor for the ecology of the ocean; it is more like a web where one species might be at a low level during its first life stage, being potential food for the elders of its own kind, and then moving up as it gets older. At each stage in the chain there are many different, competing species. Establishing and quantifying these relations is an enormous task and one that will always be surrounded with uncertainty. It comes as no surprise, therefore, that even in the most thoroughly studied ecosystems such as the Barents Sea there are enormous gaps in our knowledge. Even there the interrelations among species are only partly taken into account in fisheries management. We know that cod eats capelin and shrimp, that young herring eat small capelin, that seals eat cod and capelin and that the polar bears eat the seals, but there is hardly any attempt at managing the fish stocks as a part of this whole. The only way in which this is done is that when setting catch quotas for capelin on the basis of stock assessment the scientists involved try to take into account how much of the capelin will be eaten by the cod and make sure that enough capelin will be left to breed after the fishing season is over.

Yet there is a voluminous literature devoted to ecosystem-based fisheries management. Typically this literature is short on quantification or even rudimentary information on ecosystem relations, but what is lacking in scientific rigor is more than made up by verbosity. More often than not it turns out that ecosystem-based management is something quite different from an intelligent and informed food production from the sea; instead it is new gloss put on an environmental agenda, such as preserving "iconic" animals like sea lions or whales. As these animals need food to support themselves, the question arises to what extent their maintenance comes at the expense of our food production. Ecosystem management worthy of its name would try to establish this in a scientific way, but that is seldom if ever done.

Some scientists, such as Alan Fitzsimmons in his book *Defending Illusions*, even think that ecosystem management is empty of meaning. He dismisses popular phrases such as ecosystem health, ecosystem integrity, ecosystem management, and ecosystem sustainability as meaningless slogans and points out that there is no single, agreed, and objective way to define an ecosystem; there is a plethora of definitions depending on the user's need and preference. He is concerned with ecosystems on land, but his arguments would seem to be even more applicable to marine ecosystems.

An early example of an ecosystem management issue is the development of the anchovy fishery in Peru. The Peruvian guano industry saw the anchovy fishery as a threat. Hordes of sea birds preyed on the anchovy and deposited their waste products on islands off the shore of Peru, which was then dug out by the guano industry and exported all over the world as fertilizer. Much space need not be spilled on the question what made most sense from the point of view of efficiency, "capturing" the anchovy in the form of bird droppings shipped away as fertilizer to grow cereals, perhaps eaten by pigs, or catching the anchovy directly and turning it into feed for pigs and poultry. The guano industry was dying in any case and did not make much headway with its opposition. This was well before the plethora of environmental organizations that now push the case of sea birds and other animals as parts of sacred nature. Chances are that they would have joined hands with the guano industry and thwarted the anchovy fishery.

Another issue under the theme of ecosystem management is the "fishing down the food chain" hypothesis. It is alleged that our fishing industry has severely decimated the top predators, so that more and more of the fish in the ocean is at low levels in the food chain. There are indeed reasons why this might have happened, and there is some evidence that it has in fact happened.

As already mentioned, the most coveted fish is often relatively high up in the chain, and the incentives for depleting such species in an open access fishery would be strong. On the other hand, it is not clear that fishing down the food chain would necessarily be bad; if we are concerned with getting as much biomass as possible from the oceans we should eliminate the top predators and have our fishing fleet catching the fish further down in the chain. When biomass is passed from a lower level to a higher level in the food chain a large part of it, probably 80–90 percent, is lost in the transfer, because the predator fish need energy to maintain themselves and to search for and capture their prey. Furthermore, all the biomass that the predator fish would turn into net growth would never be available to our fishing fleets.

Due to the notion of ecosystem management where some fish or animal species are valued as such and not as sources of food or materials, it has become popular to put a value on them in that capacity. The approach is perfectly sensible from a logical point of view. Consider a fish like a sardine which we can capture from the sea. The value of this captured fish is derived from its use as input for the fish meal industry or as feed for tuna fattening or as bait in a sports fishery (but seldom as food for humans). This value is reflected in the market price; the particular use able to pay the highest price will get the sardine, and typically all of them are able to get some. This is not so for the value of the sardine if left in the sea. This value is no less real and stems from several sources. First, there is the value of the sardine as fish that can grow and reproduce; if they were all taken out there would be none in the next season. Then there is the value of the sardine as feed for other wild fish that we might catch. Finally there is the value of the sardine as feed for animals such as sea lions that we might value as a part of nature. There is no market that reflects these values; they would have to be derived from numerical models reflecting the ecological relations involved. The knowledge of these ecological relations is too rudimentary to make this anything but a very inexact science.

But the value of sardines as feed for sea birds and sea lions poses additional problems. First, does it make sense to evaluate the effect on wildlife on a weight unit basis? Probably not; people probably care about viability of herds of wild animals while valuing an additional pound of sea lions probably makes little sense. Then there are the methodological problems associated with eliciting the implied values from those who care about these animals. These are so-called contingent values; they are nowhere observed in any market and people must be asked about them. The problems here have to do with the fact that the respondents never part with the money they say they are willing to pay, as discussed in chapter 4.

BRENT SPAR

Does anyone still remember Brent Spar? It was one of those hyperboles that flash over the television screens and the tabloid front pages with great fanfare and then are quickly forgotten.[9] It was a campaign against polluting the oceans, but one based on misconceptions and misrepresentations. It is worthy of mentioning as a warning of the excesses that ill informed environmentalist campaigns may result in.

So what was Brent Spar and what was the fuss all about? Brent Spar was an oil tank floating on the sea and used for storing oil from the Brent oil field in the North Sea, before it was pumped into tankers and transported away. It was owned by the oil company Shell. By the early 1990s it had served its purpose and was to be scrapped. Shell's engineers had made a careful study of how to dispose of it and found that the cheapest and least harmful way was to sink it into the Atlantic at a depth of 2,000 meters. At such depth there is little marine life to be harmed, and the harmful substances that might leak out of the tank would do so over a long time and be greatly diluted by the vast volume of ocean surrounding it.

But such was not to be. Greenpeace found a "good" case to campaign for. They sent their activists on board the tank where they chained themselves to the mast. Removal was difficult and attracted the media. In the meantime Greenpeace managed to build up a case about pollution of the ocean, which was hardly an issue. The gullible public was led to believe that the oil tank was to be scuttled into the North Sea, where it would have been more of a threat than where it was intended to be, a couple of kilometers down in the Atlantic.

A major propaganda war resulted. Facts gave way to the powers of the imagination, fueled by reported half-truths. Greenpeace presented its own facts, which turned out to be fiction. Shell's gas stations were boycotted; in Germany a Molotov cocktail was thrown at one of them. In the end Shell abandoned its plans.

But what to do with the tank? Dismantling it was by no means without its own hazards; in fact, that was the very reason why it was to be scuttled in the first place. The tank, even if empty of oil, was full of residues and hazardous gases. In the end a Norwegian shipyard undertook to take it apart. It was towed into a fjord in Norway where it was cut up. The operation took several months. Several times a fire broke out, but every time it was quickly put out and no explosions occurred. The cost was formidable, but the material found good use; it came to its final rest as a quayside in the vicinity of Stavanger.

NOTES

1. Smith et al. (2010), p. 274.

2. See Baumgartner, T. R., A. Soutar, and V. Ferreira-Bartrina (1992): Reconstruction of the history of Pacific sardine and northern anchovy populations over the past two millennia from sediments of the Santa Barbara Basin, California. *California Cooperative Oceanic Fisheries Investigations Reports* 33:24–40.

3. FAO (2012), p. 53.

4. See FAO (2012), figure 18.

5. There were in fact two alternative proposals, one by New Zealand and the United States, and one by France, the European Union, and Australia. Both serve a similar purpose and are supported by similar arguments.

6. See FAO (2009).

7. Source: The International Fishmeal and Fish Oil Organisation (www.iffo.net), *Fishmeal and Fish Oil Statistical Yearbook.*

8. See Tacon, Albert G. J., and Marc Metian (2008): Global overview on the use of fish meal and fish oil in industrially compounded aquafeeds: Trends and future prospects. *Aquaculture* 285: 146–58.

9. Shortly afterwards a book was published about Brent Spar (Rice and Owen, 1999).

Chapter Nine

Conclusion

The integrated nature of the world means that it may soon be possible to capture the entire world on behalf of a foolish idea. . . . The wrong kind of chiefs, priests and thieves could yet snuff out future prosperity on earth.

—Matt Ridley (2010), pp. 357–58

Again and again over the past quarter century, after people see the data showing that all trends pertaining to human welfare have been improving rather than deteriorating—health, welfare, education, leisure, availability of natural resources, cleanliness of our air and water . . . . [W]hy, then, do our media and our political leaders tell us the opposite. . . . [W]hy do we hear that there is need to "save the planet"?

—Julian Simon (1999), p. 117

Cassandra's curse was to foresee the future but never to be believed. For the modern environmental prophets it is the opposite, the believers stand ready. Consider this:[1]

We already know it is too late to reverse the planet's transformation, and we know what is going to happen next—superstorms, super-droughts, super-pandemics, massive population displacement, water scarcity, desertification and all the rest. Massive destruction, displacement and despair. Our worst fears are already upon us. The reality is far worse than anyone has imagined.

Who speaks with such conviction? Nathaniel Rich, a novelist. He is para-phrased by Peter B. Kelemen, an earth scientist and self-acknowledged mem-ber of the climate-consensus community. But professor Kelemen's take on the climate problem is considerably more moderate, not to say optimistic. He fully acknowledges the immense uncertainty surrounding the global warming issue, the extent to which it is happening, to what extent it is man-made, what the consequences could be, and what we could do about it.

Here is another sample. A group of Norwegian scientists who disagree with the "climate consensus" distributed an information brochure to schools and libraries across the country, in response to material which in their view was biased and incorrect. An indignant comment, penned by a novelist and a librarian, characterized the brochure as ". . . incorrect information which could undermine the young people's motivation to fight for their right to a sustainable future."[2] Is anthropogenic climate change a faith for sustainability warriors? Heresy is never welcome among believers.

But global warming is on hold, the gas markets are glutted, the oil is still flowing albeit expensive, population increase is on the wane, and the oceans are not being emptied of fish. There are other problems we should be paying more attention to: religious fundamentalism of a sort different from environmentalism, poverty and lack of economic development, civil wars with their attendant atrocities, curable but still neglected diseases, and functional illiteracy in our schools. The "predictions" by environmental extremists are not just harmless absurdities one can have fun with, but too often they are believed by politicians and decision makers who divert time and money to costly measures solving nonexistent problems. Is solar and wind power one such? They are not competitive, but in the best of cases these technologies could be useful at some point in the future. The ban on DDT has been characterized as an unwarranted response to an imaginary problem (the birds of America were never threatened by it) and has probably killed millions of people in malaria-infested parts of the world.[3]

The cure for this is science, uncorrupted and free of advocacy, science that is based on facts and tests theories against observations, not science that is used selectively to support faiths and worldviews adopted a priori. Science looks for evidence, in particular evidence that may disprove established theories and notions. That can be an arduous and ungratifying process. In 2001 a young, Danish statistician, Bjørn Lomborg, created a lot of stir by publishing a book entitled *The Skeptical Environmentalist*. It was a systematic attempt to debunk a series of environmental myths by contrasting them with the facts. Several popular environmentalist tenets were addressed; that the world's forests and fish stocks are being rapidly depleted; that living species are going extinct on an unprecedented scale; that we are living on borrowed time, as some environmentalists would have us believe; that we are depleting our resources, both renewable and non-renewable, on such a scale that our future existence is threatened; that the pollution of our environment is contributing to the same end. Lomborg found this difficult to reconcile with the seemingly obvious fact that our living standards are consistently rising, not least in countries that not so long ago were in abject poverty and by many considered cases beyond redemption.

Ironically, Lomborg set out to disprove Julian Simon's contention that the world had by and large gotten better on most quantifiable accounts over the years. In his last book, published posthumously, Simon speaks as a disillusioned man. He notes that the Lord held out a severe punishment for those prophets who made false predictions. From Deuteronomy: ". . . the prophet that shall speak a word presumptuously in My name, which I have not commanded him to speak, . . . that prophet shall die," to which Simon added: "The newspapers and television take a different view of prophesy about the environment, resources, and population growth. False performance over the past 30 years at least has been rewarded with ever-greater attention by the press. And correct forecasting has not brought greater attention and respect by the press; mostly, it has brought obloquy."[4]

Lomborg followed in the footsteps of Simon, but more thoroughly, and painstakingly considered a variety of sources: statistics about the extent of forests, about abundance of fish stocks, about species extinctions, deposits of oil and minerals, and many other things. His conclusions were for the most part that various assessments by environmentalists were biased, selective, and inaccurate, and sometimes even more faith-based than fact-based. His overall assessment was that mankind on the whole is on the right track and making progress and far from jeopardizing its own future.

His book caused an uproar among environmentalists. Several world famous ones of that crowd published a letter in *Scientific American* (January 2002) trying to refute the book. There were attempts to have the publisher, Cambridge University Press, withdraw it from the market, in the best tradition of the Inquisition. In Denmark, Lomborg's home country, he was accused of unethical scientific practice. A panel on scientific ethics ruled in his disfavor, finding that he used sources selectively in order to prove his points rather than presenting a balanced view. The panel's support of its conclusion was not convincing; it bore all the hallmarks of political correctness. In the end it had no consequences whatever.

The allegation of selective use of sources raises a few questions. Are we to understand that the paragons of environmentalism never engage in that kind of activity? Even a casual reading of their books and articles makes one doubt. But what does selective use of sources mean, and what kind of a crime is it? We can take our cue from court proceedings and even science itself. Advocates argue the case of their clients; they present evidence and arguments favorable to the client's case. That is a perfectly legitimate process as long as they stick to facts and do not present evidence they know is false. An unbiased judgment indeed requires that all facts and arguments be presented, and that is why there are both prosecutors and defenders. If a "balanced view" is supposed to be some average of all views, ill or well taken, let us rather have good judgment based on all available and valid evidence. In science, theories survive only as long as they cannot be disproved. To dispose of erroneous theories one looks for evidence that can disprove them.

Lomborg's book has to be seen in that light. Lomborg was trying to refute the multifaceted environmental hypothesis that things are going from bad to worse on our planet. He looked for evidence that might go against hypotheses such as species are disappearing at an alarming and unprecedented rate, that the forests of the planet are rapidly shrinking and fish disappearing from the oceans, and that we have less and less left of oil and minerals. The evidence concerning many of these questions is complicated, contradictory, and difficult to interpret, but what many environmentalists did not like was presentation of evidence contrary to their apparently strongly held beliefs. Lomborg carefully documented his sources and was never accused of falsifying or misreporting anything. But he set out to disprove certain statements. The Danish council of ethics in science seems to have missed that point. What would disqualify Lomborg is if he used sources and evidence he knew was false and unreliable. In the absence of that, dismissing Lomborg's book is to dismiss freedom of speech and intellectual inquiry, something characteristic of those who know that they and they alone know the truth and have the insights. Too often that is an adequate description of environmental activists, even scientists acting in that capacity.

As a case in point, consider the influential book *Silent Spring*, by many considered the primary inspiration for the environmental movement. Here's what the biographer of Rachel Carson, the author of *Silent Spring*, has to say on this point: "Carson was not always neutral in her use of sources and . . . she was sometimes driven by moral fervor more than by scientific evidence. Indeed, her use of evidence was selective, and she made no attempt to catalogue the benefits of pesticides. . . ."[5] This does not make intentional selectivity in the use of evidence by Bjørn Lomborg any better, to the extent it did occur, but environmentalists ought to be the first to admit that he would be sinning in good company.

This book makes no pretense of replicating Lomborg's work. His statistics are, of course, getting outdated, but the sources are given for anyone who wishes to update them and check their validity and whether or not trends have persisted. Instead I have pointed out the dubious philosophical pedigree of environmentalism, its anti-human bias, and its destructive implications for our civilization and our way of life. But there is good and there is bad in environmentalism; there are those who just want to take care of nature in our own interest and call themselves environmentalists in that capacity. It seems, however, that the ecofundamentalists have come a long way in capturing this nice-sounding phrase for themselves so that those with more moderate opinions and wishing to promote a wise use of nature should perhaps consider other words to describe their attitudes, in order not to be associated with the tree huggers, the crusaders against fossil fuels, and the whale worshippers.

Bjørn Lomborg called himself a skeptical environmentalist. The ire and opprobrium heaped upon him speaks volumes about the unfortunate and unwarranted influence of extreme environmentalism. But we should not be surprised. In the evangelical environmentalist circles there is no room for skepticism. All evangelicals know how to save the world. But would we want to destroy civilization in order to save the world? Hopefully not. By and large, and especially since the industrial revolution, mankind has made enormous progress; with our technology we have made this planet of ours a better place. There is every reason to believe that our progress from good to better can continue for a long time to come, particularly if those of our fellow human beings afflicted by environmentalist delusions can get them out of their heads.

NOTES

1. From Dot Earth, the *New York Times*, April 27, 2013.
2. See their website, www.klimarealistene.com.
3. See *Three Speeches by Michael Crichton*, Science and Public Policy Institute, December 2009, and *Silent Spring at 50* (2012; eds.: Meiners, Roger, Pierre Desrochers, and Andrew Morriss).
4. Simon (1999), p. 117.
5. Lytle (2007), p. 220.

Literature

Anderson, Terry L. and Henry I. Miller (eds.; 2000): *The Greening of U.S. Foreign Policy*. Hoover Institution Press, Stanford.

Bolch, Ben and Harold Lyons (1993): *Apocalypse Not*. The Cato Institute, Washington D.C.

Brink, Patrick ten (ed., 2011): *The Economics of Ecosystems and Biodiversity in National and International Policy Making*. Earthscan, London and Washington D.C.

Brown, Lester (1970): *Seeds of Change*. Praeger, New York.

Brown, Lester (2008): *Plan B 3.0: Mobilizing to Save Civilization*. W.W. Norton & Company, New York.

Bryce, Robert (2010): *Power Hungry*. Public Affairs, New York.

Carson, Rachel (1962): *Silent Spring*. Houghton Mifflin, Boston.

Demarest, Arthur (2010): *Ancient Maya*. Cambridge University Press, Cambridge, U.K.

Diamond, Jared (2006): *Collapse*. Penguin, London.

Donlan, C.J. et al., "Pleistocene rewilding: an optimistic agenda for twenty-first century conservation," in Richard J. Ladle (ed., 2009): *Biodiversity and Conservation*. Routledge, London, pp. 447–85.

Ehrlich, Paul R. (1968): *The Population Bomb*. Ballantine Books, New York.

Ehrlich, Paul A. and Ann H. Ehrlich (1974): *The End of Affluence*. Ballantine Books, New York.

Ehrlich, Paul A. and Ann H. Ehrlich (1991): *The Population Explosion*. Touchstone, New York.

FAO (2009): Fish as feed input for aquaculture. *FAO Technical Paper* 518. Food and Agricultural Organisation of the United Nations, Rome.

FAO (2012): *The State of World's Fisheries and Aquaculture*. Food and Agricultural Organisation of the United Nations, Rome.

Fitzsimmons, Allan K. (1999): *Defending Illusions*. Rowman & Littlefield, New York.

Gibbon, Edward (1993/1776–1778): *The Decline and Fall of the Roman Empire*. With an Introduction by Hugh Trevor-Roper. Everyman's Library, Alfred A. Knopf, New York.

Goklany, Indur M. (2001): *The Precautionary Principle*. Cato Institute, Washington D.C.

Griffin, Keith (1979): *The Political Economy of Agrarian Change*. Macmillan, London.

Haq, Gary and Alistair Paul (2012): *Environmentalism since 1945*. Routledge, London.

Helm, Dieter (2012): *The Carbon Crunch*. Yale University Press, New Haven.

Huggins, Laura L. and Hanna Skandera (eds., 2004): *Population Puzzle. Boom or Bust?* Hoover Institution Press, Stanford, California.

Idso, Craig, Robert M. Carter and S. Fred Singer (eds., 2011): *Climate Change Reconsidered, 2011 Interim Report*. The Heartland Institute, Chicago.

Jevons, William Stanley (1906/1865): *The Coal Question*. Third Edition, with a foreword by A.W. Flux. Macmillan, London.

Kaufman, Wallace (1994): *No Turning Back*. toExcel, Lincoln, Nebraska.

Ladle, Richard J. (ed., 2009): *Biodiversity and Conservation*. Routledge, London.

Lomborg, Bjørn (2001): *The Sceptical Environmentalist*. Cambridge University Press, Cambridge.

Lytle, Mark Hamilton (2007): *The Gentle Subversive*, Oxford University Press, Oxford.

MacKay, David J.C. (2009): *Sustainable Energy without the Hot Air*, www.withouthotair.com.

Malthus, Thomas (1999/1798): *An Essay on the Principles of Population*. Edited with an introduction and notes by Geoffrey Gilbert. Cambridge University Press, Cambridge.

Marx, Karl and Friedrich Engels (1998/1848): *The Communist Manifesto*. Edited with an introduction and notes by David McLellan. Oxford University Press, Oxford.

McWilliams, James E. (2009): *Just Food*. Back Bay Books, New York.

Meadows, Donella H., Dennis L. Meadows, Jørgen Randers and William W. Behrends III (1972): *The Limits to Growth*. New American Library, New York.

Meiners, Roger, Pierre Desrochers and Andrew Morriss (eds.; 2012): *Silent Spring at 50*. Cato Institute, Washington D.C.

Michaels, Patrick J. and Robert C. Balling, Jr. (2009): *Climate of Extremes*. Cato Institute, Washington D.C.

Miller, Henry I. (1997): *Policy Controversy in Biotechnology: An Insider's View*. Academic Press, San Diego, California.

Miller, Tyler G. Jr. (1998): *Living in the Environment*, Wadsworth, Belmont, California.

Morriss, Andrew P., William T. Bogart, Roger E. Meiners and Andrew Dorchak (2011): *The False Promise of Green Energy*. Cato Institute, Washington D.C.

Myrdal, Gunnar (1968): *Asian Drama*. An Inquiry into the Poverty of Nations. Allen Lane: Penguin Press, London.

Nelson, Robert H. (1991): *Reaching for Heaven on Earth*. Rowman & Littlefield, Savage, Maryland.

Nelson, Robert H. (2010): *Economic vs. Environmental Religion: The New Holy Wars*. Penn State Press, University Park, Pennsylvania.

Ninnan, K.N. (ed., 2009): *Conserving and Valuing Ecosystem Services and Biodiversity*. Earthscan, London.

Rice, Tony and Paula Owen (1999): *Decommissioning the Brent Spar*. Routledge, London.

Ridley, Matt (2010): *The Rational Optimist*. Fourth Estate, London.

Sheehan, James M. (2000): "Sustainable Development: The Green Road to Serfdom?" In Anderson, Terry L. and Henry I. Miller (eds.), pp. 143–165.

Simon, Julian (1999): *Hoodwinking the Nation*. Transaction Publishers, New Brunswick (USA) and London.

Singer, S. Fred and Avery, Dennis T. (2007): *Unstoppable Global Warming*. Rowman and Littlefield, New York.

Smith, Michael H., Karlson "Charlie" Hargroves, and Cheryl Desha (2010): *Cents and Sustainability*. Earthscan, London and Washington D.C.

Sondergaard, Steven E. (2009): *Climate Balance*. Tate Publishing & Enterprises, Mustang, Oklahoma.

Sunstein, Cass R. (2002): *Risk and Reason*. Cambridge University Press, Cambridge U.K.

Truett, Joe C. and Stephen R. Johnson (eds., 2000): *The Natural History of an Arctic Oil Field*. Academic Press, San Diego, California.

Vogt, William (1948): *Road to Survival*. Sloane, New York.

Weisman, Alan (2007): *The World Without Us*. St. Martin's Press, New York.

Westad, Odd Arne (2012): *Restless Empire*. The Bodley Head, London.

World Commission on Environment and Development (1987): *Our Common Future*. Oxford University Press, Oxford.

Wyler, Rex (2004): *Greenpeace*. Rodale, London.

Index

About the Author

Rögnvaldur Hannesson was born and raised in Iceland. He received his Ph.D. in economics at the University of Lund, Sweden. He was professor of fisheries economics at the Norwegian School of Economics in Bergen from 1983 until 2013, when he retired at the age of 70. He has published six books on the economics of fisheries, petroleum and mineral wealth, and close to 100 articles, mainly on fisheries and resource economics, in refereed journals.

CPSIA information can be obtained at www.ICGtesting.com
Printed in the USA
BVOW09*1647110214

344522BV00006B/9/P